COMBINATION MICROWAVE COOKING TIMES AND RECIPES

COMBINATION MICROWAVE COOKING TIMES AND RECIPES

Bernice Hurst

foulsham

LONDON • NEW YORK • TORONTO • SYDNEY

ACKNOWLEDGEMENTS

I would like to offer my thanks to the many people who offered advice and information on combination cooking: Belling & Co Ltd, Panasonic UK Ltd and Siemens Domestic Appliances for lending ovens on which the recipes were tested; Jones & Brother, Hitachi Sales UK Ltd, Samsung Electronics (UK) Ltd and Sanyo Marubeni (UK) Ltd for copies of their own recipe and instruction books.

Photographer Mike O'Neill
Home Economist Janet Warren
The Publishers would like to thank Panasonic UK Ltd for the loan of an oven for photography

foulsham

Yeovil Road, Slough, Berkshire SL1 4JH

ISBN 0-572-01528-3

Printed in Great Britain by
St Edmundsbury Press Ltd, Bury St Edmunds, Suffolk

CONTENTS

CONVERSION TABLES

As conversions cannot always be exact, we recommend that you follow one set of measurements only. Please note that when using American measurements the volume of ingredients can vary, therefore 1 cup of flour actually weighs less than 1 cup of sugar and may not look equivalent to the Metric and Imperial measurements given.

Dry Measurements

Metric	*Imperial*	*American*
5 ml	1 tsp	1 tsp
15 ml	1 tbsp	1 tbsp
25 g	1 oz	1 oz
125 g	4 oz	¼ lb
225 g	8 oz	½ lb
450 g	1 lb	1 lb
1 kg	2.2 lb	2.2 lb

Liquid Measurements

Metric	*Imperial*	*American*
5 ml	1 tsp	1 tsp
15 ml	1 tbsp	1 tbsp
25–30 ml	1 fl oz	2 tbsp
50–60 ml	2 fl oz	¼ cup
250 ml	8 fl oz	1 cup (½ pint)
300 ml	½ pint	1¼ cups
450 ml	¾ pint	1 pint
575 ml	1 pint	2½ cups
1 litre	1¾ pints	4½ cups

INTRODUCTION

Combination microwave ovens are one of the newest additions to the kitchen market. As microwave ovens become standard equipment, manufacturers are taking things one step further. Because, labour and time saving though they may be, microwave ovens alone remain supplements to standard ovens. There are tasks with which microwave ovens simply cannot cope.

Not so combination ovens. It is only this new generation which can do everything — and more — that both traditional and microwave ovens can. By combining the features of traditional and microwave ovens, combination ovens achieve the best possible results in the quickest way possible. The conventional and microwave functions can be used separately, alternately or simultaneously to offer a variety of cooking methods.

The aim of this book is to demonstrate and explain the use of combination ovens. It will show you how to adapt your own, favourite, recipes as well as offering a selection of dishes to broaden your combination range. For those of you with a copy of *Fan Oven Cooking Times and Temperatures*, a few of the recipes will look familiar. Several have been repeated in this book deliberately to show the ease with which you can convert from fan oven and conventional cooking to combination cooking. You will see how they have been adapted to make the best use of the different functions and to produce excellent results whichever cooking method you select. There are no recipes for microwave cooking on its own, but plenty using microwaves on a combination mode plus entire dishes cooked on combination.

Cooking with a combination oven is not difficult, but it is different. It requires patience to deal with the initial complexities, but once mastered, should achieve quick, efficient and delicious results every time. Read the next few pages carefully as they will answer many of your questions to ensure that you become a proficient combination cook with the minimum of effort and confusion.

COMBINATION COOKING EXPLAINED

What is a combination oven?

Combination ovens contain a combination of functions consisting of microwaves plus the addition of convection heat either via a fan, conventional top and bottom elements, a grill or halogen lamps. Some ovens include more than one of these features. An explanation of the choices available of these combinations is given on page 9.

Most of the ovens are the size of a large microwave oven and sit on a shelf or work surface, but some manufacturers are now making full-size, built-in combination ovens. With these multifunction combination ovens you have every conceivable alternative in one full-sized unit. Their main disadvantage is that you can only use one type of cooking at a time i.e. you cannot combination cook one dish while grilling another. With all combination ovens, strict time-tabling is essential for meal planning.

What can combination ovens do and how?

Combination ovens can do everything a microwave oven can do PLUS everything that a conventional oven can do PLUS a number of unique things possible only because the combination of functions exists. Chief among the latter is simultaneous browning, crisping and high speed cooking. Until now, microwaves could not compete with conventional ovens for crisping and browning but conventional ovens could not compete with microwaves for speed.

These alternatives exist because the various functions can be used separately or simultaneously. If, for instance, you are cooking fish or vegetables, the microwave function can be used on its own. If you are baking scones or biscuits, the convection function is best. But if you want a quick cake or roast with a golden finish or crispy topping then the combination function is perfect. Whether your oven contains a fan, a grill, conventional top and bottom elements or halogen lamps, these external sources of heat balance the internal fast-cooking by the microwave for superb results in the minimum amount of time.

How do I choose?

All combination cookers can be used to cook by microwaves alone and can also be used to cook by convection heat only. In addition there are some extra features available in some models which you may like to consider.

Size There are two sizes of combination cookers available. The work-top oven that is similar in size to a standard microwave oven, or a built-in combination cooker which is of a similar size to a conventional built-in oven and which is much more expensive than the work-top models.

Pre-set Programmes Some combination cookers have preset programmes providing a selection of different combinations of microwave energy and temperature setting for various foods. This does limit the choice of settings but you can still follow the recipes in this book, see page 12.

Two Level Cooking In some cookers there is a control which you select to ensure even cooking when using a shelf in the oven.

Sensor Some models have a sensor which can be programmed to cook food automatically by measuring the amount of moisture released.

Grill Built-in grills are available in some combination cookers which can be used with or without microwave energy.

Halogen Heat As an alternative to convection heat, halogen filaments are fitted to the top and one side of the oven and can be used alone for browning and grilling or combined with microwaves for fast cooking and crisping.

COOKING CHOICES

Best results for your favourite foods will be achieved using the programmes recommended below.

Microwave only	*Convection only*	*Combination*
fresh/frozen vegetables	biscuits	roasts
fresh/frozen fish	meringues	fish dishes
fresh/frozen fruit	small cakes/pies	vegetable dishes
steamed puddings	scones	desserts
eggs (not boiled)	batters	cakes and pastries
pasta/rice/pulses	rolls	bread
soup	soufflés	casseroles
jams/preserves	choux pastry	all baked dishes
reheating		jacket/roast potatoes
defrosting		most convenience foods

Reading through this or other books on combination cooking, you may find recipes for some of the types of dishes listed above with different cooking instructions. These will generally have been adapted to suit the cooking mode recommended but for using your own favourite recipes, it is best to follow these suggestions.

Setting times and temperatures for roasts vary widely and it is always best to follow the manufacturer's instructions for these. For best results, after cooking joints should always be wrapped in foil (shiny side in) and left to rest for 10 minutes before carving.

Never preheat an empty oven on Microwave or Combination, always set it for Convection.

If your combination oven has a grill, it should be used on its own or in grill/microwave combination for thin cuts which need to brown and cook quickly e.g. chops, beefburgers, sausages, bacon, fish fingers, kebabs, etc.

Given the wide range of options available on a combination oven, you should plan carefully to make the most of what it can offer you. The different functions can be used individually for pre-cooking and browning, cooking meals and batch baking as well as in combination for cooking whole meals or improving favourite dishes.

Meal planning will require some organisation to take full advantage of your choices. Sauces and vegetables can be slightly undercooked first on microwave only, before the oven gets hot from being used on the combination setting then reheated later. The main course and potatoes can then be cooked on combination, the sauce finished and vegetables reheated while the main course "rests" for a few minutes. Desserts can be cooked on combination or microwave while you are enjoying your meal. Standing time isn't quite so essential with combination cooking as it is with microwave cooking, but roasts and puddings especially, improve with a 5–10 minute rest before serving.

COOKING VARIATIONS

All the recipes have been thoroughly tried and tested, but a number of factors affect cooking time. Following these guidelines should reduce the margin for error.

1. Cold food will take longer to cook than food at room temperature.
2. Thick cuts will take longer to cook than thin cuts.
3. Full, deep dishes will take longer to cook than shallow dishes.
4. Meat and poultry with bones will normally take longer to cook than boneless cuts.
5. Items of similar shape and size cook faster than odd shapes. The smaller or thinner the piece of vegetable or meat, the faster it will cook.
6. Food will cook faster in round or oval dishes than in square or rectangular dishes.

Another factor which will affect your cooking is preheating time. Many ovens, particularly if they have fans, do not need to be preheated. When preheating is necessary, it rarely takes more than 5 minutes. Whether or not you preheat depends both on the oven and the result you are trying to achieve. If cooking time is short or quantities small then food may not brown or crisp sufficiently without preheating. Again, familiarise yourself with both the advice given in the individual recipes in this book and the manufacturer's instructions. Each oven is different and you will get to know your own oven and its idiosyncrasies by experience only.

One of the major differences between ovens is the amount of programming you will need to do. The microwave settings for the recipes in this book are as follows:

High = 100% full power (600 watts)
Medium = 50% power (300 watts)
Low = 30% power (180 watts)

Some ovens operate on a numerical or alphabetical system which means that you do not have to programme the different power and temperature settings but simply choose from the guide given in the instruction manual for the type of dish you are cooking. Examples might be 1 = Microwave Low 160 through 4 = Microwave Medium 200 or C1 = recommended setting for fruit cakes and pâtés through C9 = recommended setting for combination grilling.

In some combination ovens the microwave power, when using the combination mode, is set at medium (50%). If a higher microwave power is called for in the recipe, allow a little extra cooking time.

Similarly, 500 and 700-watt combination microwave ovens are available in both table-top and built-in models. If you are using a 500-watt oven your dish will require a slightly longer cooking time than that indicated in the recipes; if you are using a 700-watt oven your dish will require a slightly shorter cooking time. The only hard and fast rule to follow is – always undercook first. Estimate the time you think you need then check the food and cook for a few minutes longer if necessary. Add only a minute or two before checking again and keep checking until you are satisfied. There are so many variables – from the ingredients themselves to the size and shape of both the ingredients and the cooking containier – not to mention the fact that two models of the same oven can differ slightly as they come off the conveyor belt, that a skilled cook has got to depend on his or her own judgement. This is not as hard as it sounds. As you become more familiar with you oven, timings will come naturally.

To adapt the recipes in this book for pre-set ovens, check your instruction book for the closest programme. If you cannot find one that fits the bill exactly, choose a slightly lower microwave setting and check the timing as you go along. With any microwave cooking, whether microwave alone or combination, it is always better to under-estimate than to over-estimate the cooking time. These instructions also apply when you are adapting one of your own recipes to combination cooking.

Do not be frightened by your combination microwave oven. It may seem complicated at first, but the controls are there to make cooking easier. It rarely takes more than a few minutes to master and you can always cancel any mistakes and start again.

CORRECTING YOUR MISTAKES

food too pale or soggy — preheat the oven, increase temperature and/or increase cooking time, flash dish under grill to finish

food brown but not properly cooked — increase microwave power, decrease oven temperature, increase cooking time

food overcooked — decrease microwave power, decrease cooking time, decrease oven temperature, increase liquid if food is dried out

too much splashing — reduce microwave power and/or oven temperature, cook in deeper dish, drain fat halfway through

cracked cakes — make hollow in centre of batter before baking

bottom crust not cooked — place pie dish on preheated tray or, for open pie, bake pastry then add filling and finish baking

TAKING CARE OF YOUR OVEN

It is important to remember that combination ovens get hot. Be sure to use oven gloves when removing dishes and always let the oven cool down before you begin to clean it. For best cooking results, the oven should be cleaned after each use – a quick and easy job. A damp cloth is usually sufficent but for more stubborn marks, refer to your instruction book. Excessive splattering can be avoided by using the splash guard supplied with the oven and/or cooking fatty joints in a shallow dish.

COMBINATION COOKING: THE ADVANTAGES

Whether setting up a new home, supplementing or replacing an existing appliance, there are many reasons for selecting a combination oven. First, it produces superb food very quickly for convenience and economy in time and money. Combination and microwave cooking provide healthier food. Valuable nutrients and flavour are all retained. With this new generation oven it is now possible to produce perfect food every time, using both traditional and ultra-modern methods of cooking. Combination cooking is quick and convenient, meeting the needs of virtually anyone entering a kitchen, whether you are a skilled chef or a novice, catering for a family or single person.

CONVENIENCE FOOD COOKING

As a general rule, the times given for cooking fresh or frozen convenience foods conventionally should be halved. Use the temperature given on the pack and set the microwave function to medium for pies, meat or poultry or low for fish, cheese or egg dishes. Follow your oven manufacturer's instruction about utensils. Often foil dishes should be placed directly on the turntable or insulation mat, but this varies. It may be necessary to transfer food to serving dishes before heating. If you are cooking two dishes at the same time, be sure that they do not touch.

Use this selection of frozen dishes to adapt other convenience foods.

Dish	*Setting*	*Temperature*	*Time*
oven chips	Combination Medium	250°C	10–12 minutes
battered/crumbed fish	Combination Medium	250°C	8–10 minutes
individual pies	Combination Medium	250°C	12 minutes
fish pie (serves 4)	Combination Medium	250°C	15–18 minutes
meat pie (serves 4)	Combination Medium	250°C	15–18 minutes
chicken pie (serves 4)	Combination Medium	250°C	15–18 minutes
cottage pie (serves 2)	Combination High	250°C	15–18 minutes
chicken kiev (serves 1)	Combination Medium	230°C	20 minutes
battered/crumbed chicken	Combination Medium	250°C	8–10 minutes
lasagne (serves 2)	Combination High	250°C	10–15 minutes
moussaka (serve 2)	Combination High	250°C	10–15 minutes
pizza (2)	Combination Medium	250°C	8–10 minutes
pancake rolls (2)	Combination Medium	250°C	10 minutes
quiche/flan	Combination Medium	220°C	10–12 minutes
fruit pie (serves 4)	Combination Medium	250°C	15–18 minutes
custard tart	Combination Medium	220°C	18–20 minutes

ACCESSORIES

The accessories supplied with your oven will include all or some of those listed below. When and how to use them varies and it is important to read your manufacturer's instruction book before you start cooking.

Turntable: food cooked in an oven with a turntable does not need to be stirred as frequently as food cooked on the floor of the oven. The size and shape of dishes must be checked, however, to make sure that they fit properly on the turntable. In some ovens, when using the combination or convection functions, you can stop the turntable from rotating.

Wire racks: these can be high, medium or low and you may have more than one supplied with your oven. They are primarily used to ensure that the air circulates around the food when you are using the combination function but can also be used to cook on two levels simultaneously. The high rack is particularly useful if your oven has a grill element.

Insulating mat: supplied with those ovens where you can use metal baking tins for combination cooking. Results vary with metal tins and you will learn as you go whether or not to accept the manufacturer's recommendation.

Drip and baking trays: either round or rectangular depending on whether or not the oven has a turntable. You can use the tray for fatty meats to reduce splashing or for sitting dishes on. Sometimes food can be placed directly on the tray for baking, but check the instruction manual to be certain.

Shelf: supplied in ovens without turntables so that you can cook on two levels at once or raise dishes nearer to the heat source. If the oven has a grill element, this is particularly useful.

COOKING UTENSILS

You will find that you already have a number of utensils which are suitable for use in your combination oven so it should not be necessary to buy a lot of new equipment. The chart below is a guide to various suitable materials, but do check your instruction handbook as different manufacturers' recommendations vary. Utensils with gold, silver or other metal trim or decoration must not be used. Do not cook with metal lids on dishes.

Utensil	*Microwave*	*Convection*	*Combination*
glass (heat resistant)	Yes	Yes	Yes
lead glass	No	No	No
ceramic (glazed)	Yes	Yes	Yes
pottery/earthenware	Yes	Yes	Yes
china (heat resistant)	Yes	Yes	Yes
plastic dishes/covering	Yes	No	No
microwave ware	Yes	No	No
browning dish	Yes	No	No
boiling/roasting bags	Yes	No	No
paper/paperboard	Yes	No	No
aluminium foil containers	No	Yes	Yes
aluminium foil wrapping	*	Yes	*
metal baking tins	No	Yes	*
cast iron	No	Yes	No
wood/wicker	Yes	No	No

* Check manufacturer's instructions.

SNACKS AND STARTERS

A well chosen starter provides a contrast in texture and flavour to the courses which follow. There is a selection in this chapter to suit all occasions and more substantial ideas suitable for a light lunch or supper dish.

Page 19

Camembert en Croûte (page 20); Crab Cheese and Rice Ramekins (page 21); Barbequed Spareribs (page 21); French Onion Soup (page 24).

Baked Eggs

Preparation time
5 minutes

Cooking time
4 minutes

To serve 4

Ingredients	Metric	Imperial	American
Butter	*25 g*	*1 oz*	*2 tbsp*
Grated cheese	*225 g*	*8 oz*	*1 cup*
Eggs	*4*	*4*	*4*
Salt and pepper			
Chives	*20 ml*	*4 tsp*	*4 tsp*

Spread four individual ramekins with half of the butter. Sprinkle half of the cheese into the base of each dish. Jarlsberg, Emmenthal, Gruyère or any strong flavoured English cheese can be used.

Carefully break one egg into each ramekin. Sprinkle with salt and pepper and cover with the remaining cheese. Dot with butter. Place the ramekins in the oven, taking care that they do not touch. Bake for 4 minutes on COMBINATION MEDIUM 250°C. Place on individual serving dishes and sprinkle with snipped chives.

Camembert en Croûte

Preparation time
5 minutes

Cooking time
10 minutes plus 5 minutes standing time

To serve 2

Ingredients	Metric	Imperial	American
Puff pastry	*125 g*	*4 oz*	*¼ lb*
Camembert (round)	*1*	*1*	*1*
Egg	*1*	*1*	*1*

Roll out the puff pastry to make a large circle. Place the Camembert on top. Brush the edge of the pastry with beaten egg and fold over. Brush with egg again and ensure that the parcel is well sealed. Place seam side down on an ovenproof baking dish. Glaze the top with egg. Bake the cheese for 9 minutes on COMBINATION MEDIUM 250°C or until the pastry is well risen and golden brown. Leave to rest for 5 minutes before cutting. Serve with cranberry or redcurrant jelly.

Note: instead of puff pastry, dip the cheese into beaten eggs and breadcrumbs before baking as described above. Press the crumbs into the cheese firmly and be sure that it is thoroughly and thickly coated.

Crab, Cheese and Rice Ramekins

Preparation time
5 minutes

Cooking time
3 minutes

To serve 4

Ingredients	Metric	Imperial	American
Cooked rice	*50 g*	*2 oz*	*¼ cup*
Crabmeat	*175 g*	*6 oz*	*¾ cup*
Spring onions or	*3*	*3*	*3*
Spanish onion, chopped	*30 ml*	*2 tbsp*	*2 tbsp*
Garlic	*1 clove*	*1 clove*	*1 clove*
Mayonnaise	*30 ml*	*2 tbsp*	*2 tbsp*
Grated Gruyère cheese	*50 g*	*2 oz*	*¼ cup*
Cayenne pepper	*pinch*	*pinch*	*pinch*

Combine the rice, crabmeat, chopped onions, crushed garlic and mayonnaise. Spoon into 4 greased ramekins and sprinkle with the grated cheese and cayenne pepper. Arrange on the rack and cook for 3 minutes on COMBINATION HIGH 250°C. Serve immediately.

Hot Baked Avocados

Preparation time
10 minutes

Cooking time
10 minutes

To serve 4

Ingredients	Metric	Imperial	American
Margarine	*45 ml*	*3 tbsp*	*3 tbsp*
Plain (pastry) flour	*45 ml*	*3 tbsp*	*3 tbsp*
Milk	*300 ml*	*½ pint*	*1¼ cups*
Grated onion	*5 ml*	*1 tsp*	*1 tsp*
Tomato purée (paste)	*10 ml*	*2 tsp*	*2 tsp*
Curry powder	*5 ml*	*1 tsp*	*1 tsp*
Crabmeat	*225 g*	*8 oz*	*1 cup*
Avocados	*2 large*	*2 large*	*2 large*
Lemon juice	*15 ml*	*1 tbsp*	*1 tbsp*
Salt	*pinch*	*pinch*	*pinch*

Melt the margarine on MICROWAVE HIGH. Add the flour and mix well. Gradually add the milk, stirring constantly. Cook for 5 minutes on MICROWAVE HIGH, stirring occasionally.

Season the sauce with grated onion, tomato purée and curry powder. Add the crabmeat and mix well.

Cut the avocados in half and remove the stones. Sprinkle with lemon juice and salt. Arrange in an ovenproof dish and spoon the sauce over the avocados. Bake for 5 minutes on COMBINATION MEDIUM 250°C.

Note: prawns (shrimp) can be used instead of crabmeat.

Savoury Choux Nibbles

Preparation time
10 minutes

Cooking time
10 minutes

Makes 12 to 16

Ingredients	Metric	Imperial	American
Water	*150 ml*	*¼ pint*	*⅔ cup*
Butter	*45 ml*	*3 tbsp*	*3 tbsp*
Salt	*pinch*	*pinch*	*pinch*
Plain (pastry) flour	*65 g*	*2½ oz*	*⅔ cup*
Eggs	*2*	*2*	*2*
Cayenne pepper or chilli powder (optional)	*pinch*	*pinch*	*pinch*
Grated cheese	*50 g*	*2 oz*	*¼ cup*
Sweetcorn or chopped mushrooms or cooked ham	*125 g*	*4 oz*	*½ cup*

Place the water, butter and salt in an ovenproof bowl. Heat for 2 minutes on MICROWAVE HIGH or until the water boils.

Pour the flour into the water and mix well. Cook for 2 minutes on MICROWAVE HIGH.

Beat the eggs together; stir into the pastry a spoonful at a time, mixing well after each addition. Add the cheese and flavourings of your choice and mix well.

Drop spoonsful of pastry mixture on a flat ovenproof dish. Bake for 8 minutes on COMBINATION HIGH 250°C or until the pastries are well risen and golden.

Barbecued Spareribs

Preparation time
15 minutes

Cooking time
2 minutes

To serve 2

Ingredients	Metric	Imperial	American
Pork (Chinese) spareribs	*450 g*	*1 lb*	*1 lb*
Hoisin sauce	*50 ml*	*2 fl oz*	*¼ cup*
Soy sauce	*15 ml*	*1 tbsp*	*1 tbsp*
Dry vermouth	*15 ml*	*1 tbsp*	*1 tbsp*

Parboil the spareribs for 10 minutes. Drain well and arrange bone side up on the rack of your oven. Combine the remaining ingredients and brush half over the ribs. Cook for 10 minutes on COMBINATION LOW 220°C. Turn the ribs over, brush with the remaining sauce and cook for 10 minutes on COMBINATION LOW 220°C.

Note: cooking time will vary slightly depending on the amount of meat on the ribs.

Creamed Onion Tart

Preparation time
15 minutes

Cooking time
30 minutes

To serve 4

Ingredients	Metric	Imperial	American
Filling			
Onions	*450 g*	*1 lb*	*1 lb*
Butter	*50 g*	*2 oz*	*¼ cup*
Flour	*30 ml*	*2 tbsp*	*2 tbsp*
Paprika	*5 ml*	*1 tsp*	*1 tsp*
Single (light) cream	*300 ml*	*½ pint*	*1¼ cups*
Salt	*pinch*	*pinch*	*pinch*
Sugar	*pinch*	*pinch*	*pinch*
Pastry			
Plain (pastry) flour	*175 g*	*6 oz*	*1½ cups*
Salt	*pinch*	*pinch*	*pinch*
Margarine	*75 g*	*3 oz*	*⅓ cup*
Water	*30 ml*	*2 tbsp*	*2 tbsp*

Peel and thinly slice the onions. Place in an ovenproof dish with the butter, cover and cook for 10 minutes on MICROWAVE HIGH or until the onions are tender. Add the flour and paprika and mix well. Slowly add the cream, stirring constantly. Season to taste with salt and sugar.

Combine the flour and salt for the pastry. Rub in the margarine until the mixture resembles coarse breadcrumbs. Bind to a dough with the water. Roll out and line a 20 cm/8 inch flan dish. Prick the base with a fork.

Pour the onion sauce into the pastry base. Bake for 20 minutes on COMBINATION LOW 200°C. If your oven does not have a fan, preheat before baking the tart.

Note: This recipe can be varied by using different vegetables. Cauliflower broken into small florets is delicious, particularly if the filling is sprinkled with grated cheese. Thinly sliced peppers can be used and also sliced courgettes, or use a mixture of vegetables.

Sweet Potato Soup

Preparation time
15 minutes

Cooking time
20 minutes

To serve 6

Ingredients	Metric	Imperial	American
Butter or margarine	*50 g*	*2 oz*	*¼ cup*
Chopped onion	*1*	*1*	*1*
Sweet potatoes	*450 g*	*1 lb*	*1 lb*
Tomato pureé	*15 ml*	*1 tbsp*	*1 tbsp*
Ham or beef stock	*1 litre*	*2 pints*	*5 cups*
Salt and pepper			
Single cream	*50 ml*	*2 fl oz*	*¼ cup*
Chopped fresh parsley	*45 ml*	*3 tbsp*	*3 tbsp*

Melt the butter or margarine on MICROWAVE HIGH in a deep ovenproof dish. Add the onion, mix well, cover and cook for 3 minutes on MICROWAVE HIGH.

Peel and chop the sweet potatoes. Add to the onion along with the tomato pureé and stock. Cover and cook for 15 minutes on COMBINATION HIGH 250°C. Check that the potatoes are soft and cook for a few minutes longer if necessary. Cool slightly then pureé. Season to taste with salt and pepper.

Reheat in a covered bowl on MICROWAVE HIGH. Serve with a swirl of cream and a sprinkling of parsley.

French Onion Soup

Preparation time
15 minutes

Cooking time
30 minutes

To serve 4

Ingredients	Metric	Imperial	American
Onions	*450 g*	*1 lb*	*1 lb*
Butter	*50 g*	*2 oz*	*¼ cup*
Ham or beef stock	*1¼ litres*	*2 pints*	*5 cups*
Bay leaf	*1*	*1*	*1*
Sugar	*pinch*	*pinch*	*pinch*
Salt and pepper	*pinch*	*pinch*	*pinch*
French bread	*4 slices*	*4 slices*	*4 slices*
Grated Gruyère cheese	*60 ml*	*4 tbsp*	*4 tbsp*

Peel and thinly slice the onions. Place in a large casserole with the butter, cover and cook for 10 minutes on MICROWAVE HIGH. The onions should be very soft.

Add the stock, bay leaf, sugar, salt and pepper to the onions. If you are using ham stock, omit the salt. Mix well, cover and cook for 15 minutes on MICROWAVE HIGH. Mix well, remove the bay leaf and adjust the seasoning.

Arrange the bread on top of the casserole, sprinkle with cheese and cook for 5 minutes on COMBINATION MEDIUM 250°C or until the cheese is bubbly and golden.

Flaky Spinach Pies

Preparation time
15 minutes

Cooking time
15 minutes

To serve 4

Ingredients	Metric	Imperial	American
Olive oil	*30 ml*	*2 tbsp*	*2 tbsp*
Fresh spinach	*450 g*	*1 lb*	*1 lb*
Lemon juice	*30 ml*	*2 tbsp*	*2 tbsp*
Salt			
Feta cheese	*125 g*	*4 oz*	*½ cup*
Cumin seeds	*5 ml*	*1 tsp*	*1 tsp*
Filo pastry	*2 sheets*	*2 sheets*	*2 sheets*
Melted butter	*50 ml*	*2 fl oz*	*¼ cup*

Place the olive oil in an ovenproof dish. Wash the spinach, drain well and add to the oil. Cover and cook for 5 minutes on MICROWAVE HIGH. Cool slightly then chop.

Mix the spinach with lemon juice, salt to taste, diced cheese and cumin seeds.

Cut each sheet of pastry in half. Brush each piece of pastry with melted butter and spread the spinach mixture over the bottom third. Fold to make parcels, place in a shallow ovenproof dish and brush with melted butter. Bake for 8 minutes on COMBINATION MEDIUM 250°C or until the pastry is crisp and golden. Serve hot or cold.

Note: filo pastry can be filled with any combination of ingredients to make large or small pies for starters, snacks or main courses. Always brush liberally with butter to ensure that the pastry is crisp once it is baked.

VEGETABLES AND VEGETARIAN DISHES

The quick cooking in little additional liquid which is possible in a microwave ensures that vegetables retain their colour, fresh taste, texture and nutritional value. With a combination cooker you can also achieve crisp toppings.

Page 27

Potato Kugel (page 28); Leeks and Bacon Mornay (page 33); Okra with Hot and Sweet Peppers (page 37); Spinach and Cheese Pie (page 31).

Buttered New Potatoes

Preparation time
5 minutes

Cooking time
15 minutes

To serve 4–6

Ingredients	Metric	Imperial	American
New potatoes	*900 g*	*2 lb*	*2 lb*
Water	*60 ml*	*4 tbsp*	*4 tbsp*
Butter	*125 g*	*4 oz*	*½ cup*

Wash the potatoes well and arrange in a single layer in an ovenproof casserole. Add the water and dot with butter. Cover and cook on the rack for 15 minutes on COMBINATION HIGH 200°C. Turn the potatoes over halfway through the cooking time.

Potato Kugel

Preparation time
15 minutes

Cooking time
25–30 minutes

To serve 4

Ingredients	Metric	Imperial	American
Potatoes	*900 g*	*2 lb*	*2 lb*
Onion	*1 large*	*1 large*	*1 large*
Eggs	*2*	*2*	*2*
Salt and pepper			
Matzoh meal or flour	*45 ml*	*3 tbsp*	*3 tbsp*

Peel and grate the potatoes and onion. Mix thoroughly with the eggs, salt and pepper and matzoh meal or flour. Spread in a well greased flan dish. Bake for 25 minutes on COMBINATION LOW 200°C.

Serve the Kugel hot with apple sauce and roast chicken or pork.

Note: cooking time will depend on the depth of your baking dish. The recommendation above will produce a shallow Kugel with a crisp topping. For a softer Kugel, use a deeper dish and allow a few minutes extra to cook through.

Scalloped Potatoes

Preparation time
15 minutes

Cooking time
25 minutes

To serve 4

Ingredients	Metric	Imperial	American
Margarine	*50 g*	*2 oz*	*¼ cup*
Salt	*2½ ml*	*½ tsp*	*½ tsp*
Garam masala	*15 ml*	*1 tbsp*	*1 tbsp*
Tomatoes, chopped	*225 g*	*8 oz*	*½ lb*
Potatoes	*225 g*	*8 oz*	*½ lb*
Cauliflower	*1 medium*	*1 medium*	*1 medium*

Melt the margarine on MICROWAVE HIGH. Stir in the salt, garam masala and tomatoes.

Peel the potatoes and cut into large chunks. Whole new potatoes can also be used. Mix with the tomatoes in a large ovenproof casserole. Cover and cook for 10 minutes on COMBINATION HIGH 250°C.

Cut the cauliflower into sprigs. Add to the casserole, mix well, cover and cook for 10 minutes on COMBINATION HIGH 250°C.

Note: the cooking time may vary slightly depending on how soft you like the vegetables.

Cauliflower Bhajji

Preparation time
15 minutes

Cooking time
20 minutes

To serve 4

Ingredients	Metric	Imperial	American
Butter	*125 g*	*¼ lb*	*½ cup*
Potatoes	*900 g*	*2 lb*	*2 lb*
Salt and pepper			
Single (light) cream	*575 ml*	*1 pint*	*2½ cups*
Grated Gruyère cheese	*125 g*	*4 oz*	*¼ lb*

Use half of the butter to grease a shallow ovenproof dish.

Wash, peel and thinly slice the potatoes. Arrange in layers, sprinkling each layer with salt and pepper. Pour the cream and grated Gruyère cheese over the top then dot with the remaining butter. Cook for 25 minutes on COMBINATION MEDIUM 220°C.

Note: finely chopped or thinly sliced onions can also be scattered over each layer of potatoes.

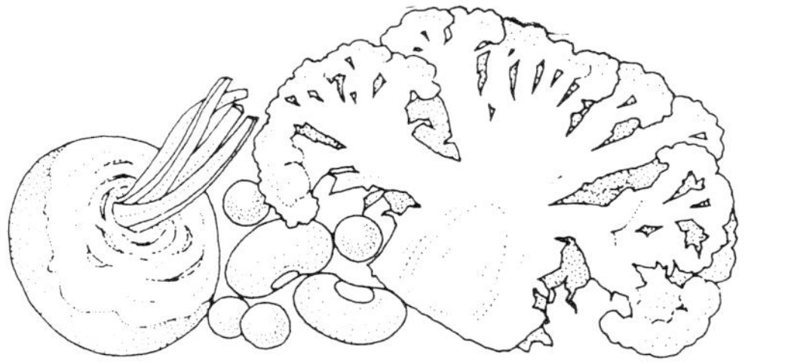

Baked Tomatoes

Preparation time
15 minutes

Cooking time
5–7 minutes

To serve 4

Ingredients	Metric	Imperial	American
Tomatoes	*4 large*	*4 large*	*4 large*
Salt	*5 ml*	*1 tsp*	*1 tsp*
Breadcrumbs	*125 g*	*4 oz*	*1 cup*
Dried basil or	*5 ml*	*1 tsp*	*1 tsp*
Fresh basil	*10 ml*	*2 tsp*	*2 tsp*
fresh parsley	*30 ml*	*2 tbsp*	*2 tbsp*
Garlic	*2 cloves*	*2 cloves*	*2 cloves*
Olive oil	*60 ml*	*4 tbsp*	*4 tbsp*

Choose very firm tomatoes, wipe with a damp cloth and cut in half across the width. Scoop out the seeds, sprinkle the shells with salt and turn upside down to drain for 10 minutes.

Combine the breadcrumbs, chopped herbs and crushed garlic. Add just enough oil to moisten but leave the filling crumbly.

Turn the tomatoes right side up and arrange in a shallow ovenproof dish. Fill with the stuffing mixture and drizzle the remaining oil over the top. Bake for 5 minutes on COMBINATION MEDIUM 250°C.

Note: cooking time may vary slightly depending on the size of the tomatoes, but do not allow them to collapse. The shells should remain firm.

Brussels Sprouts with Shallots

Preparation time
10 minutes

Cooking time
15 minutes plus
5 minutes resting time

To serve 3–4

Ingredients	Metric	Imperial	American
Brussels sprouts	*450 g*	*1 lb*	*1 lb*
Shallots	*225 g*	*8 oz*	*½ lb*
Chicken stock	*250 ml*	*8 fl oz*	*1 cup*

Clean and trim the sprouts. Peel the shallots. Place both in an ovenproof dish, pour over the stock and cook for 15 minutes on COMBINATION HIGH 250°C. Leave to rest for 5 minutes before serving.

Note: cooking time may vary slightly according to the size of the sprouts and the degree of tenderness you prefer.

Spinach and Cheese Pie

Preparation time
25 minutes

Cooking time
20 minutes

To serve 4–6

Ingredients	Metric	Imperial	American
Fresh spinach	*225 g*	*8 oz*	*½ lb*
Olive oil	*15 ml*	*1 tbsp*	*1 tbsp*
Puff pastry	*225 g*	*8 oz*	*½ lb*
Potatoes	*2 medium*	*2 medium*	*2 medium*
Onion	*½*	*½*	*½*
Tomatoes (optional)	*2*	*2*	*2*
Chopped cooked ham or bacon (optional)	*50 g*	*2 oz*	*¼ cup*
Grated cheese	*50 g*	*2 oz*	*¼ cup*
Egg	*1*	*1*	*1*

Wash the spinach well, shake off any excess water and place in an ovenproof dish with the olive oil. Cover and cook for 5 minutes on MICROWAVE HIGH. Cool and chop.

Cut the pastry into two pieces, one twice as large as the other. Roll out the larger piece to make a circle. Line the base and sides of a glass pie dish. Press the pastry firmly into the base and leave the top overlapping the edge of the dish.

Peel and thinly slice the potatoes. Cut the onion in half and slice thinly so that you have semi-circles. Arrange alternate layers of potatoes, spinach and onions in the pastry base. Season each layer with salt and pepper. If you are using tomatoes, ham or bacon divide these between the layers.

Spread grated cheese over the top layer of ingredients. You can use Emmenthal, Gruyère, Cheddar or any other strong cheese available. Mozzarella also makes a delicious alternative.

Roll out the remaining piece of pastry to make a circle slightly larger than the pie dish. Brush the edges of the pastry with beaten egg, place the lid on the pie and press gently to seal. Trim the pastry and roll out its trimmings to make decorations for the top of the pie. Brush these and the top of the pie with beaten egg to glaze. Bake for 12 minutes on COMBINATION MEDIUM 250°C or until the pastry is well risen and golden.

Mushroom Crumble

Preparation time
20 minutes

Cooking time
15 minutes

To serve 4

Ingredients	Metric	Imperial	American
Mushrooms	*450 g*	*1 lb*	*1 lb*
Garlic	*3 cloves*	*3 cloves*	*3 cloves*
Butter	*125 g*	*4 oz*	*½ cup*
Chopped onion	*30 ml*	*2 tbsp*	*2 tbsp*
Breadcrumbs	*50 g*	*2 oz*	*½ cup*
Dried parsley, basil or marjoram	*5 ml*	*1 tsp*	*1 tsp*
Parmesan cheese	*15 ml*	*1 tbsp*	*1 tbsp*

Wash and quarter the mushrooms. Crush one clove of garlic. Place the mushrooms, garlic and half of the butter in a deep, ovenproof dish. Cover and cook for 5 minutes on MICROWAVE HIGH.

Chop the remaining garlic and place in an ovenproof dish with the remaining butter and the onion. Cook for 2½ minutes on MICROWAVE HIGH.

Add the breadcrumbs, herbs and cheese to the onions. Mix well and spread evenly over the mushroom mixture. Cook for 7 minutes on COMBINATION HIGH 250°C or until the crumbs are crisp and golden.

Note: the crumble can be varied by using a combination of different varieties of mushrooms, or by adding a few dried mushrooms, soaked for 30 minutes in boiling water then sliced.

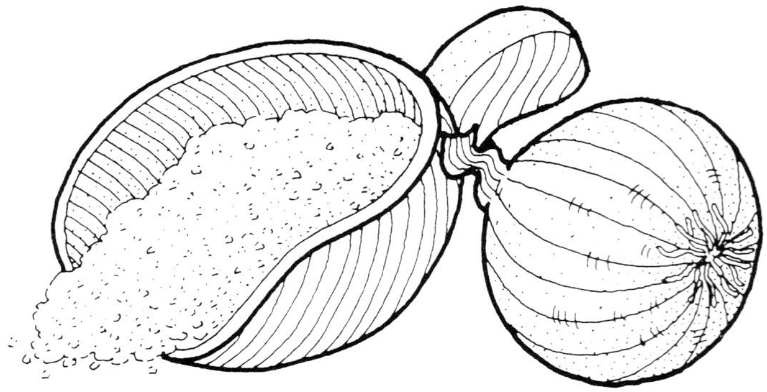

Leeks and Bacon Mornay

Preparation time
10 minutes

Cooking time
20–25 minutes

To serve 4

Ingredients	Metric	Imperial	American
Leeks	*4*	*4*	*4*
Streaky bacon	*4 rashers*	*4 rashers*	*4 rashers*
Margarine	*30 ml*	*2 tbsp*	*2 tbsp*
Flour	*45 ml*	*3 tbsp*	*3 tbsp*
Milk	*300 ml*	*½ pint*	*1¼ cups*
Salt and pepper			
Grated cheese	*50 g*	*2 oz*	*¼ cup*
Hardboiled eggs	*4*	*4*	*4*

Cut the leeks in half lengthways, trim, wash and slice. Place in an ovenproof dish with a few spoonsful of water, cover and cook for 8 minutes on MICROWAVE HIGH. Drain and set aside.

Cut the bacon across its width into strips. Place in a shallow ovenproof dish with the margarine and cook for 3 minutes on COMBINATION HIGH 250°C. Stir the flour into the bacon and slowly add the milk, stirring constantly. Cook for 5 minutes on MICROWAVE HIGH, stirring once. Adjust seasoning, add the cheese and mix well. Cook for 1 minute on MICROWAVE HIGH.

Slice the hardboiled eggs and arrange in a layer on top of the leeks. Pour over the bacon sauce and cook for 5 minutes on COMBINATION HIGH 250°C. Serve with rice.

Note: this basic recipe can be varied in countless ways. Cooked ham, meat, chicken or fish can replace the bacon and any other vegetables you like can be added. The sauce is especially delicious flavoured with a small spoonful of mustard.

Cannelloni

Preparation time
35 minutes

Cooking time
20 minutes

To serve 6

Ingredients	Metric	Imperial	American
Lasagne noodles or cannelloni tubes	*225 g*	*8 oz*	*½ lb*
Ricotta cheese	*225 g*	*8 oz.*	*½ lb*
Egg	*1*	*1*	*1*
Garlic	*1 clove*	*1 clove*	*1 clove*
Fresh parsley	*30 ml*	*2 tbsp*	*2 tbsp*
Dried basil	*10 ml*	*2 tsp*	*2 tsp*
Salt	*pinch*	*pinch*	*pinch*
Sugar	*pinch*	*pinch*	*pinch*
Tomato sauce	*575 ml*	*1 pint*	*2½ cups*
Grated Gruyère or Parmesan cheese	*60 ml*	*4 tbsp*	*4 tbsp*

Cook the lasagne noodles or cannelloni tubes as usual and spread out in a single layer on a clean tea towel to cool.

Beat the ricotta cheese with the egg until smooth and creamy. Add the chopped garlic and half of the parsley. Mix well.

Add the remaining parsley, basil, salt and sugar to the tomato sauce. This can either be home-made from your favourite recipe or, for convenience, use canned or bottled tomato sauce or Passata. If you are using home-made tomato sauce, adjust the seasonings to taste. If you prefer a spicy sauce, one or two fresh or dried chillis can be chopped and added.

Pour half of the sauce over the base of a large, shallow, ovenproof dish. The cannelloni must be cooked in a single layer, so it may be necessary to use two dishes.

To assemble the cannelloni, divide the cheese mixture equally between the sheets of noodles if using lasagne. Spread evenly and gently fold the two longer sides into the centre to make a tube shape. If using cannelloni, fill tubes with a teaspoon. Arrange in the baking dish, top with the remaining sauce and sprinkle with grated cheese. Bake for 20 minutes on COMBINATION MEDIUM 200°C.

Baked Italian Omelette

Preparation time
3 minutes

Cooking time
10 minutes

To serve 2

Ingredients	Metric	Imperial	American
Eggs	*4*	*4*	*4*
Milk	*90 ml*	*6 tbsp*	*6 tbsp*
Dried oregano	*pinch*	*pinch*	*pinch*
Parmesan cheese	*15 ml*	*1 tbsp*	*1 tbsp*
Salt and pepper			
Butter or margarine	*50 g*	*2 oz*	*¼ cup*
Chopped onion	*30 ml*	*2 tbsp*	*2 tbsp*
Fresh green chilli, chopped	*1*	*1*	*1*
Chopped mushrooms or green pepper	*45 ml*	*3 tbsp*	*3 tbsp*

Whisk the eggs until they are thoroughly blended. Add the milk, oregano, Parmesan and salt and pepper. Mix well and set aside.

Place the butter or margarine and finely chopped vegetables in a large, shallow glass pie or flan dish. Cook for 4 minutes on MICROWAVE HIGH.

Pour the egg mixture over the vegetables. Cook for 6 minutes on COMBINATION HIGH 250°C or until the eggs have set. The time may vary slightly according to the depth of the dish, so keep a careful watch on the omelette and remove when there is just a slight amount of liquid left in the very centre. Rest the omelette for a minute or two or cool completely before serving.

Note: cooked peas and potato cubes can also be added to the vegetable mixture before pouring over the eggs.

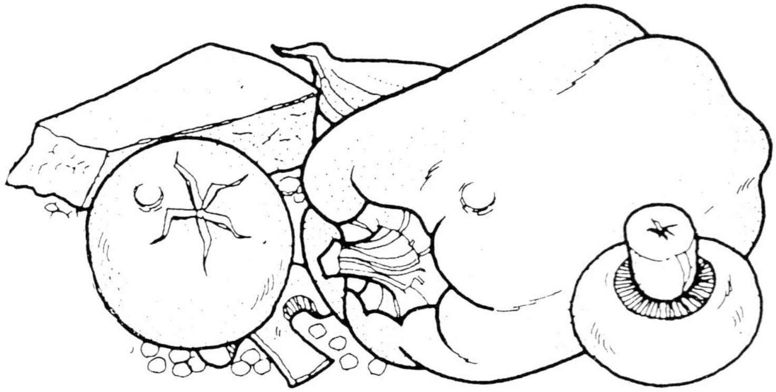

Okra with Hot and Sweet Peppers

Preparation time
10 minutes

Cooking time
25 minutes

To serve 4

Ingredients	Metric	Imperial	American
Oil or ghee	*30 ml*	*2 tbsp*	*2 tbsp*
Mustard seeds	*5 ml*	*1 tsp*	*1 tsp*
Cumin seeds	*5 ml*	*1 tsp*	*1 tsp*
Coriander seeds	*5 ml*	*1 tsp*	*1 tsp*
Black onion seeds	*5 ml*	*1 tsp*	*1 tsp*
Fresh green chillis	*1–2*	*1–2*	*1–2*
Red pepper	*1*	*1*	*1*
Green pepper	*1*	*1*	*1*
Okra	*250 g*	*½ lb*	*½ lb*
Salt	*2½ ml*	*½ tsp*	*½ tsp*

Heat the oil or ghee for 3 minutes on MICROWAVE HIGH. Add the seeds and cook for 2 minutes on COMBINATION HIGH 250°C.

Slice the chillis, which can be seeded or not according to taste. Dice the peppers, discarding seeds and core. Wash the okra well, remove the ends and cut into halves or thirds depending on their size. Mix the chillis, peppers and okra into the hot spices. Cover and cook for 20 minutes on COMBINATION MEDIUM 160°C. Stir occasionally. Serve with rice or dhal as a starter or a vegetable dish.

Braised Aubergine

Preparation time
10 minutes

Cooking time
30 minutes

To serve 4–6

Ingredients	Metric	Imperial	American
Olive oil	*50 ml*	*2 fl oz*	*¼ cup*
Garlic	*2 cloves*	*2 cloves*	*2 cloves*
Fresh green chillis	*1–2*	*1–2*	*1–2*
Aubergine (eggplant)	*450 g*	*1 lb*	*1 lb*
Mushrooms	*225 g*	*½ lb*	*½ lb*
Dried basil	*5 ml*	*1 tsp*	*1 tsp*
Dried oregano	*5 ml*	*1 tsp*	*1 tsp*
Salt	*5 ml*	*1 tsp*	*1 tsp*
Tomatoes	*450 g*	*1 lb*	*1 lb*

Heat the oil for 3 minutes on MICROWAVE HIGH. Slice the garlic and chillis, add to the oil and cook for 2 minutes on COMBINATION HIGH 250°C. The chillis can be seeded or not according to taste.

Cut the aubergine in half lengthways and then slice. Add to the garlic and chillis, cover and cook for 15 minutes on COMBINATION HIGH 220°C. Stir occasionally.

Slice the mushrooms and add to the aubergine along with the herbs and salt. Cover and cook for 5 minutes longer on COMBINATION HIGH 220°C. Stir well.

Peel and chop the tomatoes or use chopped, canned tomatoes. Add to the aubergine, mix well and cook for 5 minutes on COMBINATION HIGH 220°C.

Serve the braised aubergine with pasta or use for a vegetable lasagne.

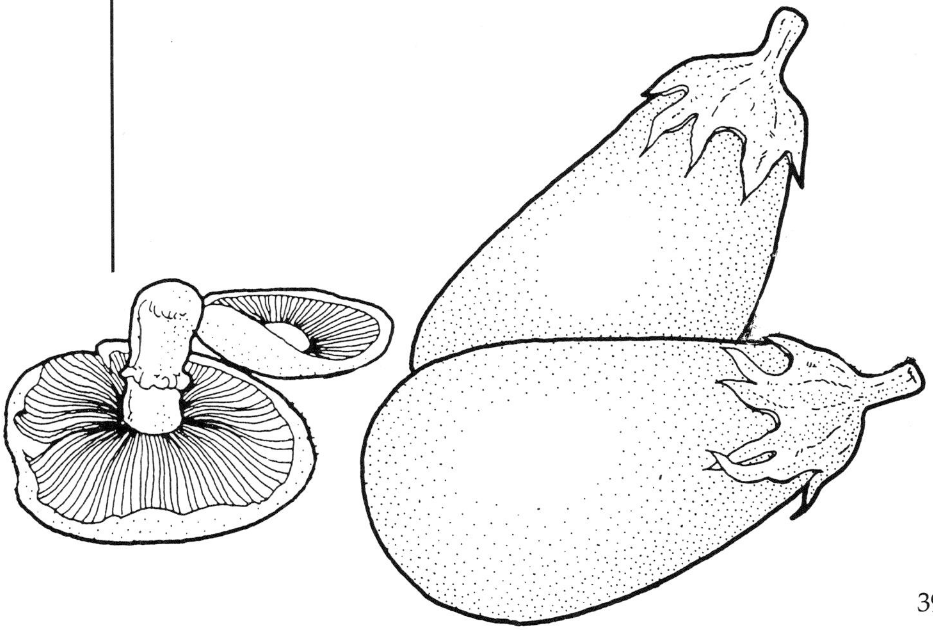

Barley and Mushroom Risotto

Preparation time
5 minutes

Cooking time
35 minutes

To serve 4–6

Ingredients	Metric	Imperial	American
Butter or margarine	*50 g*	*2 oz*	*¼ cup*
Onion	*1*	*1*	*1*
Mushrooms	*225 g*	*8 oz*	*½ lb*
Pearl barley	*225 g*	*8 oz*	*½ lb*
Vegetable or chicken stock	*450 ml*	*¾ pint*	*2 cups*

Place the butter or margarine, finely chopped onion and quartered or chopped mushrooms in a large glass baking dish. Cook for 5 minutes on MICROWAVE HIGH.

Add the barley, stir well and pour over the stock. Cover and cook for 30 minutes on COMBINATION MEDIUM 190°C, stirring occasionally. If necessary, add extra liquid if the risotto dries out before the barley is tender.

Note: the risotto will be particularly tasty if you use a combination of several varieties of mushrooms, e.g. button, oyster, shitaki or chestnut mushrooms. A few dried mushrooms, soaked for 30 minutes in boiling water and then sliced will also add interest. The soaking liquid can be used to replace part of the stock.

Lemon Carrots

Preparation time
5 minutes

Cooking time
10–15 minutes

To serve 4

Ingredients	Metric	Imperial	American
Butter or margarine	*30 ml*	*2 tbsp*	*2 tbsp*
Carrots (medium-sized)	*8*	*8*	*8*
Grated lemon rind	*15 ml*	*1 tbsp*	*1 tbsp*
Chopped fresh parsley	*15 ml*	*1 tbsp*	*1 tbsp*

Melt the butter or margarine in an ovenproof dish on MICROWAVE HIGH.

Peel and thinly slice the carrots. Toss in the melted butter, cover and cook for 10 minutes on COMBINATION HIGH 250°C. Cooking time will depend on how deeply the carrots are piled in the dish. Sprinkle with lemon rind and chopped parsley immediately before serving.

Note: grated orange rind may be used instead of the lemon rind and chopped fresh chervil or fennel may be used instead of parsley.

Variation: for candied carrots, add 15 ml/1 tablespoon each of brown sugar and honey for the last 5 minutes of cooking time and omit lemon rind and parsley.

Baked Courgettes

Preparation time
10 minutes

Cooking time
10–12 minutes

To serve 4

Ingredients	Metric	Imperial	American
Butter or margarine	*30 ml*	*2 tbsp*	*2 tbsp*
Courgettes	*8*	*8*	*8*
Sultanas	*15 ml*	*1 tbsp*	*1 tbsp*
Pine kernels	*15 ml*	*1 tbsp*	*1 tbsp*
Capers	*15 ml*	*1 tbsp*	*1 tbsp*
Salt and pepper			
Fresh basil	*6 leaves*	*6 leaves*	*6 leaves*
Chopped tomatoes	*225 g*	*8 oz*	*1 cup*
Parmesan cheese	*15 ml*	*1 tbsp*	*1 tbsp*

Place the butter or margarine in a deep ovenproof dish and melt on MICROWAVE HIGH.

Rinse the courgettes and remove the ends. Slice into rounds. Toss in the melted butter, cover and cook for 5 to 10 minutes on COMBINATION HIGH 250°C. Cooking time will depend on how deeply the courgettes are piled in the dish.

Sprinkle the sultanas, pine kernels, capers, a little salt and pepper and torn basil leaves over the courgettes. Pour over the tomatoes and top with Parmesan cheese. Cook for 3 minutes on COMBINATION HIGH 250°C.

FISH AND SEAFOOD

The moist heat of microwave cooking is the perfect way to retain the delicate flavour of fish. When cooked using the combination mode the fish is moist and flaky but any toppings or coatings become crisp and golden.

Fillet of Sole with Prawn Butter (page 44); Creole Gumbo (page 45); Herbed Monkfish (page 51).

Fillet of Sole with Prawn Butter

Preparation time
15 minutes

Cooking time
20 minutes

To serve 4

Ingredients	Metric	Imperial	American
Unsalted butter	*175 g*	*6 oz*	*¾ cup*
Button mushrooms	*125 g*	*4 oz*	*¼ lb*
Fresh sorrel or spinach	*handful*	*handful*	*handful*
Shelled prawns (shrimps)	*50 g*	*2 oz*	*¼ cup*
Lemon juice	*22 ml*	*1 ½ tbsp*	*1 ½ tbsp*
Sole or plaice (flounder) fillets	*4*	*4*	*4*
Salt and pepper			
Dry white wine	*125 ml*	*4 fl oz*	*½ cup*
Vermouth	*50 ml*	*2 fl oz*	*¼ cup*
Double (heavy) cream	*150 ml*	*¼ pint*	*⅔ cup*
Unsalted butter	*50 g*	*2 oz*	*¼ cup*

Melt a third of the butter in a shallow dish on MICROWAVE HIGH. Add the washed and chopped mushrooms, cover and cook for 3 minutes on MICROWAVE HIGH. Remove the mushrooms and reserve. Add the sorrel or spinach to the butter in the dish cover and cook for 4 minutes on MICROWAVE HIGH. Whisk thoroughly or purée.

Prepare the prawn butter by mincing the prawns and mixing well with another third of the butter, softened. Sharpen with a few drops of lemon juice.

Spread the prawn butter evenly over the fish fillets, roll up and arrange in a single layer in a buttered dish. Sprinkle with salt and pepper. Pour over the wine, cover with buttered paper and cook for 6 minutes on COMBINATION HIGH 250°C. Carefully remove the fish and set aside.

Strain the juices from the fish onto the sorrel or spinach. Add the reserved mushrooms and the vermouth and 15 ml/1 tablespoon lemon juice. Heat for 2 minutes on MICROWAVE HIGH. Season to taste. Stir in the cream and heat for 1 minute on MICROWAVE HIGH. Whisk in the remaining butter and spread a few spoonsful of sauce over the fish. Pass the remaining sauce separately.

Creole Gumbo

Preparation time
20 minutes

Cooking time
20 minutes

To serve 4–6

Ingredients	Metric	Imperial	American
Red pepper	*½*	*½*	*½*
Green pepper	*½*	*½*	*½*
Celery	*1 stick*	*1 stick*	*1 stick*
Onion	*1*	*1*	*1*
Garlic	*2 cloves*	*2 cloves*	*2 cloves*
Margarine	*50 g*	*2 oz*	*¼ cup*
Mixed cod and haddock	*450 g*	*1 lb*	*1 lb*
Flour	*45 ml*	*3 tbsp*	*3 tbsp*
Okra	*125 g*	*4 oz*	*¼ lb*
Tomatoes, chopped	*450 g*	*1 lb*	*1 lb*
Tabasco sauce	*few drops*	*few drops*	*few drops*
Prawns (shrimp)	*225 g*	*8 oz*	*½ lb*

Seed and chop the peppers. Dice the celery. Peel and chop the onion and garlic. Place all the vegetables, with the margarine, in an ovenproof dish. Cover and cook for 5 minutes on MICROWAVE HIGH.

Skin and dice the fish. Toss in the flour then mix with the softened vegetables.

Wash the okra, remove the stem and cut in half or quarters according to size. The smaller the okra, the more tender they will be. Add to the fish and mix well. Stir in the tomatoes and Tabasco sauce to taste. Cover and cook for 10 minutes on COMBINATION HIGH 250°C.

Stir the prawns into the gumbo and cook for 3 minutes on COMBINATION HIGH 250°C. Adjust seasoning and serve with rice.

Smoked Haddock Cobbler

Preparation time
25 minutes

Cooking time
25 minutes

To serve 4

Ingredients	Metric	Imperial	American
Smoked haddock fillet	*225 g*	*8 oz*	*½ lb*
Haddock or cod fillet	*225 g*	*8 oz*	*½ lb*
Black peppercorns	*6*	*6*	*6*
Milk	*300 ml*	*½ pint*	*1¼ cups*
Butter	*30 ml*	*2 tbsp*	*2 tbsp*
Sauce			
Butter	*30 ml*	*2 tbsp*	*2 tbsp*
Flour	*30 ml*	*2 tbsp*	*2 tbsp*
Milk			
Chopped fresh parsley	*15 ml*	*1 tbsp*	*1 tbsp*
Topping			
Margarine	*50 g*	*2 oz*	*¼ cup*
Self-raising flour	*225 g*	*8 oz*	*2 cups*
Baking powder	*15 ml*	*1 tbsp*	*1 tbsp*
Egg	*1*	*1*	*1*
Milk	*75 ml*	*5 tbsp*	*5 tbsp*

Place all the fish in an ovenproof dish. Add the peppercorns, milk and diced butter. Cover and cook for 10 minutes on COMBINATION MEDIUM 250°C or until fish flakes easily. Drain the fish, remove skin and any bones and flake. Strain the milk and set aside to use in the sauce.

Melt the butter for the sauce on MICROWAVE HIGH. Stir in the flour then gradually add the milk. Use the reserved milk plus enough fresh milk to make up to 300 ml/½ pint/1¼ cups. Cook for 5 minutes on MICROWAVE HIGH, stirring once. Add the parsley and fish. Adjust the seasoning.

Rub the margarine for the topping into the combined flour and baking powder. Add the beaten egg and just enough milk to make a soft dough. Turn onto a floured board, roll out gently and cut as for scones.

Spoon the fish and sauce mixture into an ovenproof dish large enough to hold the scones in a single layer. Arrange the scones on top of the fish. Brush with milk and bake for 10 minutes on COMBINATION MEDIUM 250°C until the scones are well risen and lightly browned.

Note: endless variations are possible. Use different fish, replace part of the milk with white wine, flavour the sauce with curry powder, vegetables or cheese and substitute mashed potatoes, puff or choux pastry for the cobbler topping.

Redcurrant Trout

Preparation time
5 minutes

Cooking time
15 minutes

To serve 2

Ingredients	Metric	Imperial	American
Trout fillets	4	4	4
Salt and pepper			
Small onion	½	½	½
Dried thyme	pinch	pinch	pinch
White wine or dry vermouth	175 ml	6 fl oz	¾ cup
Redcurrant jelly	30 ml	2 tbsp	2 tbsp

Season the trout with salt and pepper and place in a single layer in an ovenproof dish. Scatter sliced onion and thyme over the top then pour over the wine or vermouth. Cook for 10 minutes on COMBINATION HIGH 200°C. The cooking time may vary slightly according to the thickness of the fillets.

Remove the fish and keep warm. Strain the liquid and return to the baking dish. Stir in the redcurrant jelly. Cook for 5 minutes on MICROWAVE HIGH, stirring occasionally. Check the seasoning and spoon the sauce over the fish.

Trout au Blanc

Preparation time
10 minutes

Cooking time
15 minutes

To serve 4

Ingredients	Metric	Imperial	American
Trout	4	4	4
Flour	60 ml	4 tbsp	4 tbsp
Salt and pepper			
Unsalted butter	50 g	2 oz	¼ cup
Medium white wine	125 ml	4 fl oz	½ cup
Prawns (shrimp)	125 ml	4 fl oz	½ cup

Clean the fish and remove the heads and tails. Combine the flour, salt and pepper. Dredge the fish in seasoned flour. Shake off any excess flour and arrange the fish in a single layer in a shallow buttered dish. Cook the trout for 12 minutes on COMBINATION LOW 220°C, turning halfway through.

Pour the wine over the trout, sprinkle with prawns and cook for 3 minutes on COMBINATION LOW 220°C.

Haddock Provençal

Preparation time
15 minutes

Cooking time
20 minutes

To serve 4

Ingredients	Metric	Imperial	American
Red or green pepper	*1*	*1*	*1*
Garlic	*2 cloves*	*2 cloves*	*2 cloves*
Onion	*1*	*1*	*1*
Mushrooms	*125 g*	*4 oz*	*¼ lb*
Olive oil	*75 ml*	*3 fl oz*	*⅓ cup*
Haddock	*675 g*	*1½ lb*	*1½ lb*
Flour	*75 g*	*3 oz*	*¾ cup*
Salt and black or cayenne pepper			
Brandy	*60 ml*	*4 tbsp*	*4 tbsp*
Tomatoes, chopped	*4*	*4*	*4*
Tomato purée (paste)	*5 ml*	*1 tsp*	*1 tsp*
Sugar	*pinch*	*pinch*	*pinch*
Dried thyme	*pinch*	*pinch*	*pinch*
Bay leaf	*1*	*1*	*1*
White wine	*125 ml*	*4 fl oz*	*½ cup*

Discard seeds and core from pepper. Finely chop the garlic, pepper, onion and mushrooms. Place in an ovenproof dish with the oil, cover and cook for 5 minutes on MICROWAVE HIGH.

Skin the fish and cut into bite-sized pieces. Combine the flour, salt and black or cayenne pepper. Toss the fish in the flour. Add the fish to the vegetables, mix well and cook for 5 minutes on COMBINATION HIGH 250°C, stirring once.

Warm the brandy and pour over the fish. Set alight. When the flames have died down add the remaining ingredients. Mix well. Cover and cook for 10 minutes on COMBINATION HIGH 250°C.

Note: monkfish, turbot or halibut can be substituted for haddock. A few prawns can be added at the last minute as garnish. Serve the fish with either rice or triangles of bread fried in olive oil and sprinkled with chopped parsley.

Prawns with Egg and Pork Sauce

Preparation time
10 minutes

Cooking time
20 minutes

To serve 4

Ingredients	*Metric*	*Imperial*	*American*
Sauce			
Minced (ground) pork	*125 g*	*4 oz*	*¼ lb*
Garlic	*1 clove*	*1 clove*	*1 clove*
Spring onions or	*2*	*2*	*2*
minced onion	*15 ml*	*1 tbsp*	*1 tbsp*
Salt	*1¼ ml*	*¼ tsp*	*¼ tsp*
Dry sherry	*15 ml*	*1 tbsp*	*1 tbsp*
Soy sauce	*15 ml*	*1 tbsp*	*1 tbsp*
Water			
Cornflour (cornstarch)	*15 ml*	*1 tbsp*	*1 tbsp*
Eggs	*2*	*2*	*2*
Stir-fried prawns			
Garlic	*1 clove*	*1 clove*	*1 clove*
Salt	*pinch*	*pinch*	*pinch*
Oil	*15 ml*	*1 tbsp*	*1 tbsp*
Shelled prawns (shrimps)	*225 g*	*8 oz*	*½ lb*
Dry sherry	*10 ml*	*2 tsp*	*2 tsp*
Cornflour	*15 ml*	*1 tbsp*	*1 tbsp*

Place the pork in an ovenproof casserole and brown for 3 minutes on COMBINATION HIGH 250°C. Stir well. Add the crushed garlic, chopped spring onions or minced onion, salt, sherry, soy sauce and 125 ml/4 fl oz/½ cup of water. Mix thoroughly, cover and cook for 3 minutes on COMBINATION HIGH 250°C.

Combine the cornflour and 15 ml/1 tbsp water. Stir into the pork mixture and cook for 1 minute on COMBINATION HIGH 250°C. Stir and cook for a further 1 minute on COMBINATION HIGH 250°C. Add the beaten eggs and cook for a further 1 minute on COMBINATION HIGH 250°C.

To make stir-fried prawns: crush the garlic with salt and quickly stir-fry in hot oil in a frying pan until the aroma of the garlic is released. Sprinkle the prawns with sherry and cornflour, toss to coat and add to the garlic. Stir-fry for 2 minutes.

Add the prawns to the pork sauce and heat through for 1 minute on MICROWAVE HIGH. Serve with rice or as a filling for Chinese pancakes.

Poached Carp

Preparation time
5 minutes

Cooking time
10 minutes

To serve 2

Ingredients	Metric	Imperial	American
Carp steaks	*2 × 125 g*	*2 × 4 oz*	*2 × ¼ lb*
Onion	*½*	*½*	*½*
Carrot	*1*	*1*	*1*
Salt	*pinch*	*pinch*	*pinch*
Sugar	*pinch*	*pinch*	*pinch*
Water	*125 ml*	*4 fl oz*	*½ cup*

Place all the ingredients in a covered casserole and cook for 10 minutes on COMBINATION HIGH 250°C.

As an alternative, mince the carp and mix with an equal amount of minced cod or haddock. Bind with a beaten egg and either cracker crumbs or matzoh meal. Season with the salt and sugar then form into small balls. Place in a casserole with the onion, carrot and water and cook as above.

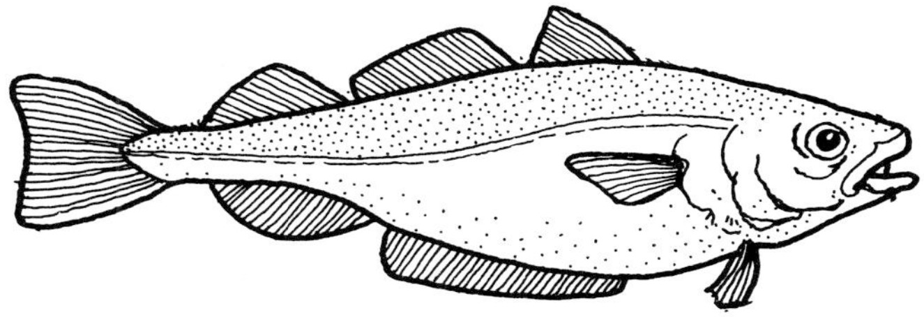

Herbed Monkfish

Preparation time
10 minutes

Cooking time
20 minutes

To serve 4

Ingredients	Metric	Imperial	American
Fresh herbs	*50 g*	*2 oz*	*2 oz*
Monkfish tail	*450 g*	*1 lb*	*1 lb*
Dry white wine	*50 ml*	*2 fl oz*	*¼ cup*

Wash the herbs and arrange in the base of a shallow ovenproof dish. Use any combination available, for instance marjoram, thyme and parsley. Place the fish on top and pour over the wine. Cover and cook for 15 minutes on COMBINATION MEDIUM 250°C. The cooking time may vary depending on the thickness of the monkfish.

Place the fish on a serving dish and keep warm. Strain the sauce and reduce by boiling rapidly until only two spoonsful are left. Pour over the fish and serve immediately with a garnish of fresh herbs. For a richer sauce, mix the reduced sauce with a spoonful of fresh cream or thick Greek yoghurt.

Cheesy Fish Steaks

Preparation time
5 minutes

Cooking time
15 minutes

•**To serve 4**

Ingredients	Metric	Imperial	American
Butter	*30 ml*	*2 tbsp*	*2 tbsp*
Flour	*30 ml*	*2 tbsp*	*2 tbsp*
Salt and pepper			
Cod steaks	*4*	*4*	*4*
Grated lemon rind	*5 ml*	*1 tsp*	*1 tsp*
Lemon juice	*15 ml*	*1 tbsp*	*1 tbsp*
Grated cheese	*60 ml*	*4 tbsp*	*4 tbsp*

Place the butter in a large, shallow ovenproof dish. Melt on MICROWAVE HIGH.

Combine the flour and a little salt and pepper. Dredge the cod steaks in seasoned flour and shake off any excess. Arrange in a single layer in the melted butter. Cook for 5 minutes on COMBINATION MEDIUM 220°C, turn carefully and cook for 5 minutes longer on COMBINATION MEDIUM 220°C.

Remove the cod steaks and stir the lemon rind and juice into the dish. Return the cod steaks to the dish and scatter grated cheese on top. Cook for 3 minutes on COMBINATION MEDIUM 250°C or flash under the grill until the cheese has melted.

Note: cooking time may vary slightly depending on the thickness of the cod steaks. Fresh or frozen cod steaks may be used. If steaks are cooked from frozen allow 3 to 4 minutes extra cooking time. Haddock steaks are also delicious cooked in this way.

Spiced Cod Steaks

Preparation time
10 minutes

Cooking time
20 minutes

To serve 4

Ingredients	Metric	Imperial	American
Olive oil	*30 ml*	*2 tbsp*	*2 tbsp*
Red pepper	*1*	*1*	*1*
Yellow pepper	*1*	*1*	*1*
Onion	*1*	*1*	*1*
Fresh green chilli	*1*	*1*	*1*
Flour	*30 ml*	*2 tbsp*	*2 tbsp*
Paprika	*pinch*	*pinch*	*pinch*
Salt	*pinch*	*pinch*	*pinch*
Cod steaks	*4*	*4*	*4*
Chopped tomatoes	*225 g*	*8 oz*	*1 cup*

Place the olive oil in a large, shallow ovenproof dish. Cut the peppers in half lengthways, remove seeds and cut into strips. Cut the onion in half and then slice. Add the vegetables to the oil and cook for 5 minutes on COMBINATION HIGH 250°C. Stir in the very finely chopped chilli.

Combine the flour, paprika and salt. Dredge the cod steaks in this mixture, shake off any excess and arrange in a single layer on top of the vegetables. Cook for 5 minutes on COMBINATION MEDIUM 220°C. Carefully turn the cod steaks over and cook for 5 minutes on COMBINATION MEDIUM 220°C. Pour over the chopped tomatoes and cook for 5 minutes more on COMBINATION MEDIUM 220°C.

Note: cooking time may vary according to the thickness of the cod steaks.

MEAT

When cooking meat in a combination microwave oven you really do have the best of both worlds. The outside of the meat becomes brown whilst the inside is tender and juicy. Meat pies and casseroles are also very successful.

Lamb Squab Pie (page 56); Meatloaf (page 64); Mexican Pork (page 64).

Lamb Squab Pie

Preparation time
15 minutes

Cooking time
40 minutes plus 10 minutes preheating time

To serve 4

Ingredients	Metric	Imperial	American
Potatoes	*900 g*	*2 lb*	*2 lb*
Onion	*1*	*1*	*1*
Cooking apples	*2*	*2*	*2*
Margarine	*125 g*	*4 oz*	*½ cup*
Salt and pepper			
Brown sugar	*5 ml*	*1 tsp*	*1 tsp*
Lamb chops or	*8*	*8*	*8*
cubed lean lamb	*900 g*	*2 lb*	*2 lb*
Chicken stock	*150 ml*	*¼ pint*	*⅔ cup*

Peel and thinly slice the potatoes. Arrange half of the potatoes in the base of a greased, shallow casserole dish.

Peel and chop the onion. Peel and chop the apples. Place in a bowl with a knob of the margarine, cover and soften on MICROWAVE HIGH for 3 minutes. Season with salt, pepper and sugar then sprinkle over the potatoes.

Place the chops or cubed lamb in an ovenproof dish with a large knob of the margarine and cook on COMBINATION HIGH 250°C for 4 minutes, stirring or turning once to seal the meat. Season with salt and pepper and arrange over the potatoes. Top with a layer of the remaining potato slices, pour over the stock and dot with the remaining margarine.

Preheat the oven for 10 minutes. Bake the lamb squab pie for 30 minutes on COMBINATION LOW 200°C.

Breast of Lamb with Spring Cabbage

Ingredients	Metric	Imperial	American
Butter	*30 ml*	*2 tbsp*	*2 tbsp*
Streaky bacon	*6 rashers*	*6 rashers*	*6 rashers*
Onion	*1*	*1*	*1*
Spring cabbage	*450 g*	*1 lb*	*1 lb*
Chopped fresh parsley	*30 ml*	*2 tbsp*	*2 tbsp*
Breadcrumbs	*75 g*	*3 oz*	*¾ cup*
Finely grated lemon rind	*5 ml*	*1 tsp*	*1 tsp*
Double (heavy) cream	*30 ml*	*2 tbsp*	*2 tbsp*
Salt and pepper			
Breasts of lamb	*2*	*2*	*2*

Preparation time
15 minutes

Cooking time
35 minutes

To serve 4

Place the butter, diced bacon and chopped onion in an ovenproof dish. Cover and cook for 5 minutes on MICROWAVE HIGH.

Shred the cabbage and add to the bacon. Mix well. Sprinkle with parsley, breadcrumbs, lemon rind, cream and salt and pepper to taste. Toss gently.

Trim as much fat as possible from the lamb and cut between the bones to make individual strips. Arrange the pieces of lamb, skin side up, on top of the cabbage. Cook for 30 minutes on COMBINATION LOW 200°C, basting occasionally with juices from the dish.

Veal Marsala

Preparation time
15 minutes

Cooking time
12 minutes

To serve 4

Ingredients	Metric	Imperial	American
Veal escalopes	*4*	*4*	*4*
Plain (all-purpose) flour	*50 g*	*2 oz*	*½ cup*
Olive oil	*30 ml*	*2 tbsp*	*2 tbsp*
Margarine	*50 g*	*2 oz*	*¼ cup*
Garlic	*1 clove*	*1 clove*	*1 clove*
Mushrooms	*125 g*	*4 oz*	*¼ lb*
Chopped fresh parsley	*30 ml*	*2 tbsp*	*2 tbsp*
Marsala	*80 ml*	*2½ fl oz*	*⅓ cup*
Chicken stock	*80 ml*	*2½ fl oz*	*⅓ cup*

Pound the veal escalopes between two sheets of greaseproof paper until they are as thin as possible. If they are too large to fit in a shallow casserole, cut them into smaller pieces.

Combine the flour, salt and pepper. Dredge the veal in flour and shake off any excess. Place the oil in a shallow ovenproof dish. Arrange the veal in the dish in a single layer if possible. Cook for 6 minutes on COMBINATION HIGH 250°C, turning once.

Place the margarine, crushed garlic and sliced mushrooms in an ovenproof dish. Cook for 2 minutes on COMBINATION HIGH 250°C. Mix in the chopped parsley.

Spread the mushroom mixture over the veal. Pour over the Marsala and stock. Cook for 3 minutes on COMBINATION HIGH 250°C to heat through.

Beef Stew with Dumplings

Preparation time
20 minutes

Cooking time
1 hour 10 minutes

To serve 4

Ingredients	Metric	Imperial	American
Stewing steak	*675 g*	*1½ lb*	*1½ lb*
Flour	*60 ml*	*4 tbsp*	*4 tbsp*
Salt and pepper			
Carrots	*4*	*4*	*4*
Shallots	*8*	*8*	*8*
Mushrooms	*8*	*8*	*8*
Oil	*45 ml*	*3 tbsp*	*3 tbsp*
Tomato purée (paste)	*30 ml*	*2 tbsp*	*2 tbsp*
Dried thyme	*5 ml*	*1 tsp*	*1 tsp*
Dried marjoram	*5 ml*	*1 tsp*	*1 tsp*
Beef stock	*300 ml*	*½ pint*	*1¼ cups*
Dumplings			
Plain (all-purpose) flour	*125 g*	*4 oz*	*1 cup*
Baking powder	*10 ml*	*2 tsp*	*2 tsp*
Sugar	*2½ ml*	*½ tsp*	*½ tsp*
Salt	*2½ ml*	*½ tsp*	*½ tsp*
Dried thyme	*5 ml*	*1 tsp*	*1 tsp*
Milk	*125 ml*	*4 fl oz*	*½ cup*

Cut the beef into cubes. Season the flour with salt and pepper. Toss the beef in the flour.

Peel the carrots and cut into thick chunks. Peel the shallots but leave whole. Wash the mushrooms and leave whole.

Put the oil, beef and vegetables in a large ovenproof casserole. Cook for 10 minutes on COMBINATION MEDIUM 250°C, stirring occasionally, to seal the meat and vegetables.

Stir in the tomato purée, herbs and salt and pepper to taste. Pour over the stock, cover and cook for 45 minutes on COMBINATION MEDIUM 220°C or until the beef is tender. Stir occasionally. Leave the stew to stand for 10 minutes.

Combine the dry ingredients for the dumplings. Add the milk and mix to a thick dropping consistency. Place spoonsful on top of the stew and cook, uncovered, for 12 minutes on COMBINATION MEDIUM 220°C or until well risen.

Note: red wine or canned tomatoes can be substituted for all or part of the beef stock.

Family Pot Roast Supper

Preparation time
10 minutes

Cooking time
1 hour 15 minutes

To serve 8–10

Ingredients	Metric	Imperial	American
Celery	*2 sticks*	*2 sticks*	*2 sticks*
Onion	*1*	*1*	*1*
Garlic	*1 clove*	*1 clove*	*1 clove*
Carrots	*2*	*2*	*2*
Oil	*30 ml*	*2 tbsp*	*2 tbsp*
Flour	*30 ml*	*2 tbsp*	*2 tbsp*
Salt and pepper	*pinch*	*pinch*	*pinch*
Paprika	*pinch*	*pinch*	*pinch*
Rolled brisket	*1¾ kg*	*4 lb*	*4 lb*
Water or canned tomatoes	*250 ml*	*8 fl oz*	*1 cup*

Finely chop the celery, onion, garlic and carrots. Place in a large casserole with the oil, cover and soften for 5 minutes on MICROWAVE HIGH.

Combine the flour, salt, pepper and paprika. Roll the brisket in seasoned flour and place on top of the vegetables. Cook for 5 minutes on COMBINATION HIGH 250°C. Turn the meat over and cook for a further 5 minutes on COMBINATION HIGH 250°C. Pour over the water, cover and cook for 1 hour on COMBINATION LOW 190°C.

Tomato Beef Stew

Preparation time
20 minutes

Cooking time
50 minutes plus 10 minutes resting time

To serve 4

Ingredients	Metric	Imperial	American
Stewing steak	*675 g*	*1½ lb*	*1½ lb*
Oil	*45 ml*	*3 tbsp*	*3 tbsp*
Flour	*30 ml*	*2 tbsp*	*2 tbsp*
Carrots	*4*	*4*	*4*
Fresh green chilli	*1*	*1*	*1*
Shallots	*6*	*6*	*6*
Mushrooms	*4*	*4*	*4*
Tomato sauce (Passata)	*450 ml*	*¾ pint*	*2 cups*
Dried basil	*5 ml*	*1 tsp*	*1 tsp*

Cut the beef into cubes. Place in a large casserole with the oil and cook for 5 minutes on COMBINATION HIGH 250°C, stirring once, to seal. Sprinkle with flour and mix well.

Peel the carrots and cut into large chunks. Seed and chop the chilli. Peel and slice the shallots. Wash and quarter the mushrooms. Add all the vegetables, tomato sauce and basil to the meat. Mix well, cover and cook for 45 minutes on COMBINATION MEDIUM 220°C or until the beef is tender. Leave to rest for 10 minutes before serving.

Basic Braised Beef

Preparation time
5 minutes

Cooking time
45 minutes plus 10 minutes resting time

To serve 6–8

Ingredients	Metric	Imperial	American
Braising steak	*900 g*	*2 lb*	*2 lb*
Shallots	*4*	*4*	*4*
Beef stock	*300 ml*	*½ pint*	*1¼ cups*
Dried thyme	*5 ml*	*1 tsp*	*1 tsp*
Coriander seeds	*2½ ml*	*½ tsp*	*½ tsp*

Leave the meat in steaks. Place in a shallow ovenproof dish and cover with sliced shallots, stock and herbs. Cover and cook for 45 minutes on COMBINATION LOW 160°C or until the meat is tender. Leave to rest for 10 minutes before serving.

This basic recipe can be varied in endless ways by adding wine or tomatoes, extra vegetables or different herbs. Once the meat is cooked, the gravy can be thickened with cornflour (cornstarch) or reduced for a concentrated sauce.

Quick Lamb Casserole

Preparation time
10 minutes

Cooking time
20 minutes

To serve 4

Ingredients	Metric	Imperial	American
Carrots	*2*	*2*	*2*
Onion	*1*	*1*	*1*
Celery	*2 sticks*	*2 sticks*	*2 sticks*
Lamb cutlets	*8*	*8*	*8*
Tomato purée (paste)	*15 ml*	*1 tbsp*	*1 tbsp*
Beef stock	*300 ml*	*½ pint*	*1¼ cups*
Rice	*125 g*	*4 oz*	*½ cup*

Peel and chop the carrots and onions. Slice the celery.

Arrange the lamb cutlets in a single layer in a shallow ovenproof dish. Brown for 5 minutes on COMBINATION MEDIUM 250°C turning once. Drain away the fat and add the carrots, onions and celery.

Dissolve the tomato purée in hot beef stock. Pour over the chops, add the rice and mix well. Cover and cook for 15 minutes on COMBINATION MEDIUM 250°C.

Note: for a quick lamb curry, add a spoonful of curry powder to the sauce and substitute a few sultanas for the vegetables.

Italian Meatball and Sausage Ragoût

Preparation time
15 minutes

Cooking time
40 minutes

To serve 8

Ingredients	Metric	Imperial	American
Italian sausages or kabanos cut into pieces	*450 g*	*1 lb*	*1 lb*
Meatballs			
White bread	*50 g*	*2 oz*	*2 oz*
Water	*50 ml*	*2 fl oz*	*¼ cup*
Minced (ground) beef	*450 g*	*1 lb*	*1 lb*
Egg	*1*	*1*	*1*
Garlic powder	*2½ ml*	*½ tsp*	*½ tsp*
Salt	*2½ ml*	*½ tsp*	*½ tsp*
Dried basil	*5 ml*	*1 tsp*	*1 tsp*
Dried oregano	*5 ml*	*1 tsp*	*1 tsp*
Dried parsley	*5 ml*	*1 tsp*	*1 tsp*
Parmesan cheese	*15 ml*	*1 tbsp*	*1 tbsp*
Sauce			
Tomato sauce (Passata)	*575 ml*	*1 pint*	*2½ cups*
Salt	*2½ ml*	*½ tsp*	*½ tsp*
Sugar	*2½ ml*	*½ tsp*	*½ tsp*
Dried basil	*5 ml*	*1 tsp*	*1 tsp*
Dried oregano	*5 ml*	*1 tsp*	*1 tsp*
Dried parsley	*5 ml*	*1 tsp*	*1 tsp*

Place the sausages in a single layer in a large ovenproof dish. Brown for 5 minutes on COMBINATION LOW 200°C, turning once or twice.

Soak the white bread in water for 5 minutes. Drain well, squeezing out all the liquid. Add to the remaining ingredients for the meatballs and mix thoroughly. Shape into small balls and arrange in a single layer in a large ovenproof dish. Brown for 5 minutes on COMBINATION LOW 200°C, turning once.

Combine all the sauce ingredients. Place the meatballs and sausages in the same pan, draining away any fat that may have accumulated. Pour over the sauce, cover and cook for 30 minutes on COMBINATION LOW 200°C. Serve with spaghetti, garlic bread and a green salad.

Mexican Pork

Preparation time
15 minutes

Cooking time
20 minutes

To serve 4

Ingredients	Metric	Imperial	American
Pork steaks	*675 g*	*1½ lb*	*1½ lb*
Oil	*15 ml*	*1 tbsp*	*1 tbsp*
Tomatoes, chopped	*225 g*	*8 oz*	*½ lb*
Chilli powder	*5 ml*	*1 tsp*	*1 tsp*
Cooked kidney beans	*225 g*	*8 oz*	*½ lb*

Cut the pork steaks into thin strips. Place in an ovenproof dish with the oil and cook for 5 minutes on COMBINATION HIGH 250°C. Stir once or twice to ensure that the meat is well sealed.

Add the tomatoes and chilli powder. Mix well, cover and cook for 10 minutes on COMBINATION HIGH 250°C.

Stir the kidney beans into the pork and heat for 5 minutes on MICROWAVE HIGH.

Serve Mexican Pork with grated Cheddar cheese, jalapeño or other pickled peppers, shredded lettuce and tortillas. Alternatively, fill enchilladas, using home-made cornmeal pancakes. Wrap the pancakes as for cannelloni, cover with a spicy tomato sauce and grated cheese then bake until the cheese has melted.

Meatloaf

Preparation time
10 minutes

Cooking time
10 minutes plus 5 minutes standing time

To serve 2

Ingredients	Metric	Imperial	American
White bread	*1 thick slice*	*1 thick slice*	*1 thick slice*
Water	*50 ml*	*2 fl oz*	*¼ cup*
Minced (ground) pork	*350 g*	*12 oz*	*¾ lb*
Egg	*1*	*1*	*1*
Fresh green chilli (optional)	*1*	*1*	*1*
Chopped fresh coriander	*15 ml*	*1 tbsp*	*1 tbsp*
Salt	*1¼ ml*	*¼ tsp*	*¼ tsp*

Soak the bread in the water for 5 minutes. Drain well, squeezing out all the liquid. Add to the pork, egg, chopped chilli, if using, coriander and salt. Mix well and shape into a loaf. Bake in a loaf dish or a shallow baking dish for 10 minutes on COMBINATION HIGH 220°C. Stand for 5 minutes.

Vary the meatloaf with different meat and spices. Serve hot or cold, on its own or with a tomato, meat, mushroom or wine sauce.

Pork with Cream Sauce

Preparation time
10 minutes

Cooking time
21 minutes

To serve 4

Ingredients	Metric	Imperial	American
Unsalted butter or olive oil	*30 ml*	*2 tbsp*	*2 tbsp*
Celery	*2 sticks*	*2 sticks*	*2 sticks*
Pork fillet or steaks	*675 g*	*1½ lb*	*1½ lb*
Chicken stock cube	*1*	*1*	*1*
Boiling water	*45 ml*	*3 tbsp*	*3 tbsp*
Dry white wine	*50 ml*	*2 fl oz*	*¼ cup*
Finely chopped			
fresh coriander or	*15 ml*	*1 tbsp*	*1 tbsp*
coriander seeds	*5 ml*	*1 tsp*	*1 tsp*
Salt and pepper			
Single (light) cream	*150 ml*	*¼ pint*	*⅔ cup*
Dijon mustard	*15 ml*	*1 tbsp*	*1 tbsp*

Melt the butter or heat the oil on MICROWAVE HIGH. Slice the celery and pork. Toss in the butter or oil and cook for 10 minutes on COMBINATION LOW 220°C.

Crumble the stock cube over the meat and celery. Add the boiling water, wine and finely chopped fresh coriander or crushed coriander seeds. Cover and cook for 10 minutes on COMBINATION LOW 220°C.

Stir in the cream and mustard. Heat for 1 minute on COMBINATION LOW 220°C.

Pork Steak Parmesan

Preparation time
15 minutes

Cooking time
15 minutes

To serve 4

Ingredients	Metric	Imperial	American
Breadcrumbs	*125 g*	*4 oz*	*1 cup*
Parmesan cheese	*30 ml*	*2 tbsp*	*2 tbsp*
Dried oregano	*10 ml*	*2 tsp*	*2 tsp*
Pork steaks	*4*	*4*	*4*
Egg	*1*	*1*	*1*
Olive oil	*30 ml*	*2 tbsp*	*2 tbsp*
Mozzarella cheese	*125 g*	*4 oz*	*¼ lb*
Tomato sauce (Passata)	*250 ml*	*8 fl oz*	*1 cup*
Sugar	*pinch*	*pinch*	*pinch*
Salt	*pinch*	*pinch*	*pinch*

Combine the breadcrumbs with half of the Parmesan cheese and half of the oregano. Dip the pork steaks into beaten egg and then into flavoured crumbs. Press the crumbs on gently and shake off any excess. Arrange the steaks in a single layer in an oiled ovenproof dish. Bake for 10 minutes on COMBINATION MEDIUM 200°C, turning once.

Slice or grate the Mozzarella cheese and arrange on top of the pork steaks.

Combine the tomato sauce, sugar, salt and remaining oregano. Pour over the pork and sprinkle with the remaining Parmesan cheese. Bake for 5 minutes on COMBINATION MEDIUM 200°C or until the Mozzarella cheese has melted.

Note: cooking time may vary depending on the thickness of the pork steaks. Rump or sirloin steak or veal escalopes can be used instead of pork steaks.

Shepherd's Pie

Preparation time
20 minutes

Cooking time
25 minutes

To serve 2

Ingredients	Metric	Imperial	American
Potatoes	*225 g*	*8 oz*	*½ lb*
Minced (ground) beef or lamb	*225 g*	*8 oz*	*½ lb*
Chopped carrot	*75 g*	*3 oz*	*⅓ cup*
Chopped onion	*30 ml*	*2 tbsp*	*2 tbsp*
Tomato purée (paste)	*5 ml*	*1 tsp*	*1 tsp*
Boiling water	*90 ml*	*6 tbsp*	*6 tbsp*
Gravy powder or	*5 ml*	*1 tsp*	*1 tsp*
stock cube	*1*	*1*	*1*
Salt and pepper			

Peel, cube and boil the potatoes. Cool and mash. Place the minced beef or lamb in a shallow ovenproof dish. Cook for 5 minutes on COMBINATION HIGH 250°C, stirring once. Add the carrot and onion and mix well.

Combine the tomato purée, boiling water and gravy powder or stock cube. Pour over the meat and vegetables. Cook for 10 minutes on COMBINATION HIGH 250°C. Season to taste. A pinch of ground cinnamon can also be added if you choose.

Spread the mashed potatoes over the cooked meat, sealing the edges well. Cook for 10 minutes on COMBINATION HIGH 250°C.

Note: to make Moussaka, prepare the meat as above and arrange in layers with browned aubergine (eggplant) slices in a casserole. Top with sautéed potato slices rather than mashed potatoes and cover with cheese sauce. Bake as for Shepherd's Pie.

Spiced Meatballs

Preparation time
15 minutes

Cooking time
15 minutes

To serve 6

Ingredients	Metric	Imperial	American
Meatballs			
Minced (ground) beef	*675 g*	*1½ lb*	*1½ lb*
Egg	*1*	*1*	*1*
Salt and pepper			
Chopped onion	*30 ml*	*2 tbsp*	*2 tbsp*
Garlic	*3 cloves*	*3 cloves*	*3 cloves*
Ground coriander	*10 ml*	*2 tsp*	*2 tsp*
Soy sauce	*15 ml*	*1 tbsp*	*1 tbsp*
Chopped fresh parsley	*15 ml*	*1 tbsp*	*1 tbsp*
Flour	*45 ml*	*3 tbsp*	*3 tbsp*
Oil	*30 ml*	*2 tbsp*	*2 tbsp*
Sauce			
Cornflour (cornstarch)	*30 ml*	*2 tbsp*	*2 tbsp*
Mango chutney	*30 ml*	*2 tbsp*	*2 tbsp*
Chicken stock cubes	*2*	*2*	*2*
Tomato purée (paste)	*10 ml*	*2 tsp*	*2 tsp*
Boiling water	*600 ml*	*1 pint*	*2½ cups*
Curry powder	*10 ml*	*2 tsp*	*2 tsp*

Combine all the ingredients for the meatballs. Mix well and shape into balls. Place in a single layer in a shallow oiled dish and cook for 5 minutes on COMBINATION HIGH 250°C.

Combine all the ingredients for the sauce. Pour over the meatballs and cook for 10 minutes on COMBINATION HIGH 250°C. Cooking time may vary slightly depending on the size of the meatballs. Serve with rice, dhal, a vegetable curry and an assortment of chutneys and pickles.

Note: make tiny bite-sized meatballs to serve with cocktails for a party nibble.

Veal and Vegetable Casserole

Preparation time
25 minutes

Cooking time
50 minutes

To serve 6

Ingredients	Metric	Imperial	American
Leek	*1*	*1*	*1*
Carrot	*1*	*1*	*1*
Celery	*1 stick*	*1 stick*	*1 stick*
Bay leaf	*1*	*1*	*1*
Fresh thyme or	*1 sprig*	*1 sprig*	*1 sprig*
dried thyme	*2½ ml*	*½ tsp*	*½ tsp*
Fresh parsley or	*6 stalks*	*6 stalks*	*6 stalks*
dried parsley	*15 ml*	*1 tbsp*	*1 tbsp*
Turnips	*3*	*3*	*3*
Shallots	*6*	*6*	*6*
Stewing veal	*900 g*	*2 lb*	*2 lb*
White wine	*125 ml*	*4 fl oz*	*½ cup*
Water	*250 ml*	*8 fl oz*	*1 cup*
Butter	*15 ml*	*1 tbsp*	*1 tbsp*
Flour	*15 ml*	*1 tbsp*	*1 tbsp*
Salt and pepper			
Egg yolk	*1*	*1*	*1*
Lemon juice	*7½ ml*	*½ tbsp*	*½ tbsp*

Clean and finely chop the leek, carrot and celery. Place in the bottom of a large ovenproof casserole. Top with herbs.

Peel and quarter the turnips. Peel the shallots but leave whole. Cut the veal into bite-sized pieces. Place the turnips, shallots and veal on top of the chopped vegetables and herbs. If possible, arrange in a single layer. Add the wine and water, cover the casserole and cook for 45 minutes on COMBINATION HIGH 190°C.

Strain off the pan juices. Keep the meat and vegetables warm.

Melt the butter on MICROWAVE HIGH. Stir in the flour and cooking liquid. Cook for 5 minutes on MICROWAVE HIGH, stirring once. Season to taste with salt and pepper.

Whisk the egg yolk with the lemon juice. Slowly pour the sauce over the egg yolk mixture, whisking constantly. Pour the sauce over the meat and vegetables. Serve with rice, sautéed mushrooms and a green vegetable.

POULTRY AND GAME

Roasting poultry and game is one of the best uses of a combination microwave oven. The meat stays moist and tender, whilst the skin becomes crisp and brown. Equally successful are made up dishes such as pies, pasta and braises.

Coriander Chicken (page 80); Braised Pheasant with Cider (page 76); Turkey and Ham Puff Pie (page 72).

Turkey and Ham Puff Pie

Preparation time
30 minutes

Cooking time
40 minutes

To serve 4–6

Ingredients	Metric	Imperial	American
Cauliflower	*225 g*	*8 oz*	*½ lb*
Broccoli	*225 g*	*8 oz*	*½ lb*
Margarine	*30 ml*	*2 tbsp*	*2 tbsp*
Flour	*30 ml*	*2 tbsp*	*2 tbsp*
Milk	*300 ml*	*½ pint*	*1¼ cups*
Grated cheese	*125 g*	*4 oz*	*½ cup*
Salt and pepper			
Cooked turkey	*125 g*	*4 oz*	*¼ lb*
Cooked ham	*125 g*	*4 oz*	*¼ lb*
Puff pastry	*450 g*	*1 lb*	*1 lb*
Egg	*1*	*1*	*1*

Wash the cauliflower and broccoli and divide into florets. Place in separate ovenproof dishes, with a few spoonsful of water in each dish. Cover and cook, one at a time, for 8 minutes on MICROWAVE HIGH. Drain, cool and chop.

Place the margarine in a jug and melt on MICROWAVE HIGH. Stir in the flour and gradually add the milk, stirring constantly. Cook for 5 minutes on MICROWAVE HIGH, stirring once halfway through. Whisk until smooth, stir in the cheese and mix well. Season to taste. Use any well flavoured English cheese, Gruyère, Parmesan or Emmenthal.

Mince the turkey and ham. Add the vegetables and sauce. Mix well and adjust seasoning to taste.

Roll out the puff pastry and trim to make a large rectangle. Set aside the unused pieces of pastry.

Spread the meat and vegetable mixture in an even column down the centre. Brush the edges of the pastry with beaten egg and fold to make a parcel. Press the edges gently to seal and turn onto a flat or shallow ovenproof dish, seam side down. Brush the surface with egg. Roll out the pastry scraps, cut into decorative shapes and arrange on top of the pie. Brush once more with egg and bake for 15 minutes on COMBINATION HIGH 250°C or until the pastry is well risen and golden brown.

Note: several smaller pies can be made if you prefer individual portions.

Chicken and Asparagus Puff Pies

Preparation time
20 minutes

Cooking time
20 minutes

To serve 2

Ingredients	Metric	Imperial	American
Fresh asparagus	*4 spears*	*4 spears*	*4 spears*
Chicken breast (cooked)	*125 g*	*4 oz*	*¼ lb*
Salt and pepper			
Double (heavy) cream	*15 ml*	*1 tbsp*	*1 tbsp*
Dijon mustard	*1¼ ml*	*¼ tsp*	*¼ tsp*
White wine	*10 ml*	*2 tsp*	*2 tsp*
Puff pastry	*125 g*	*4 oz*	*¼ lb*
Grated cheese	*30 ml*	*2 tbsp*	*2 tbsp*
Egg	*1*	*1*	*1*

Place the asparagus in an ovenproof dish with a few spoonsful of water. Cover and cook for 10 minutes on MICROWAVE HIGH. Drain and chop.

Thinly slice the chicken breast. Season with salt and pepper. Combine the cream, mustard and wine.

Divide the pastry in half and roll out thinly. Trim to make two rectangles, saving the pastry trimmings.

Divide the chicken evenly between the two rectangles, arranging it in a column down the centre. Top with asparagus and cream mixture. Sprinkle each pie with grated cheese. Use Cheddar, Emmenthal, Gruyère or anything else you like.

Fold the pastry to make neat parcels, sealing the edges well with beaten egg. Place on a greased flat ovenproof dish, join underneath. Use the reserved pastry trimmings to decorate the pies. Brush with beaten egg. Bake for 10 minutes on COMBINATION MEDIUM 250°C or until the pastry is well risen and golden brown.

Chicken Cacciatore

Preparation time
10 minutes

Cooking time
40 minutes

To serve 4

Ingredients	Metric	Imperial	American
Onion	*1*	*1*	*1*
Garlic	*1 clove*	*1 clove*	*1 clove*
Fresh green chilli	*1*	*1*	*1*
Chicken	*1 (1½ kg)*	*1 (3½ lb)*	*1 (3½ lb)*
White wine	*125 ml*	*4 fl oz*	*½ cup*

Peel and slice the onion. Peel and chop the garlic. Seed and chop the chilli. Arrange in the bottom of a large ovenproof casserole. Place the chicken, breast side down, on top of the bed of vegetables. Pour over the wine and roast for 40 minutes on COMBINATION HIGH 250°C. Turn breast side up halfway through the cooking time.

Chicken Pie with Sage Stuffing

Preparation time
20 minutes

Cooking time
25 minutes

To serve 4

Ingredients	Metric	Imperial	American
Cooked chicken	*1 (1½ kg)*	*1 (3 lb)*	*1 (3 lb)*
Cooked chipolatas	*8*	*8*	*8*
Sliced mushrooms	*125 g*	*4 oz*	*¼ cup*
Onion	*1*	*1*	*1*
Melted butter	*15 ml*	*1 tbsp*	*1 tbsp*
Breadcrumbs	*50 g*	*2 oz*	*½ cup*
Dried sage	*2½ ml*	*½ tsp*	*½ tsp*
Boiling water	*15 ml*	*1 tbsp*	*1 tbsp*
Chicken stock	*450 ml*	*15 fl oz*	*2 cups*
Flour	*15 ml*	*1 tbsp*	*1 tbsp*
Puff pastry	*125 g*	*4 oz*	*¼ lb*
Egg	*1*	*1*	*1*

Combine the diced chicken, halved chipolatas and mushrooms in a deep pie dish.

To make stuffing: slice the onion, place in a bowl of salted water and cook for 5 minutes on MICROWAVE HIGH or until soft. Drain well and mash. Mix in the melted butter, breadcrumbs and sage and stir in enough boiling water to moisten. Form into small balls and add to the dish.

Stir a spoonful of chicken stock into the flour until smooth. Blend in remaining stock. Pour over the pie.

Roll out the pastry. Cut a strip to go around the edge of the dish. Moisten slightly and cover with the large piece of pastry. Seal the edge. Prick with a fork to let the steam escape. Brush with lightly beaten egg. Bake for 20 minutes on COMBINATION MEDIUM 200°C or until the pastry is crisp and brown.

Turkey and Cranberry Pie

Preparation time
30 minutes plus 2 hours chilling time

Cooking time
15 minutes

To serve 6–8

Ingredients	Metric	Imperial	American
Pastry			
Plain (pastry) flour	*225 g*	*8 oz*	*2 cups*
Small egg	*1*	*1*	*1*
Butter	*150 g*	*5 oz*	*⅔ cup*
Salt	*2½ ml*	*½ tsp*	*½ tsp*
Sugar	*15 ml*	*1 tbsp*	*1 tbsp*
Water	*50 ml*	*2 fl oz*	*¼ cup*
Filling			
Diced cooked turkey	*300 g*	*10 oz*	*1¼ cups*
Diced cooked ham	*175 g*	*6 oz*	*¾ cup*
Cranberry sauce	*125 g*	*4 oz*	*½ cup*
Black pepper			
Egg	*1*	*1*	*1*
Chicken stock	*150 ml*	*¼ pint*	*⅔ cup*

Sieve the flour into a large mixing bowl and make a well in the centre. Break the egg into the well, add the diced butter, salt, sugar and water. Gradually draw the flour into the centre to form a dough. Mix well and then knead until smooth. (This can be done with an electric mixer or food processor.) Wrap in clingfilm and chill for 2 hours.

Cut the pastry into two pieces, one twice the size of the other. Roll out the larger piece and use to line the base and sides of a 20 cm/8 inch diameter glass pie dish. Fill with a layer of diced turkey and ham, top with cranberry sauce and finish with the remaining turkey and ham. Season to taste with black pepper.

Roll out the remaining piece of pastry. Place over the top of the pie, sealing well with beaten egg. Use any trimmings to decorate the top of the pie and glaze once more with egg. Make a hole in the top crust so that the steam can escape and insert a pastry funnel or a small roll of cardboard to keep the hole open. Bake on the rack for 15 minutes on COMBINATION HIGH 250°C.

While the pie is in the oven, boil the chicken stock rapidly until it reduces to just a few spoonsful. Slowly pour into the baked pie and leave to cool.

Variation: fill the pie with any combination of poultry, meat or vegetables. Try, for instance, pork and apple; veal, ham and egg; chicken with sautéed leeks and mushrooms; salmon, rice, hardboiled eggs and dill seeds.

Braised Pheasant with Cider

Preparation time
20 minutes

Cooking time
1 hour

To serve 4

Ingredients	Metric	Imperial	American
Apples	*4*	*4*	*4*
Onions	*2*	*2*	*2*
Celery	*2 sticks*	*2 sticks*	*2 sticks*
Butter	*75 g*	*3 oz*	*⅓ cup*
Pheasant	*2*	*2*	*2*
Plain (all-purpose) flour	*75 g*	*3 oz*	*¾ cup*
Chicken stock	*250 ml*	*8 fl oz*	*1 cup*
Cider	*250 ml*	*8 fl oz*	*1 cup*
Salt and pepper			
Bouquet garni	*1*	*1*	*1*
Double (heavy) cream	*150 ml*	*5 fl oz*	*⅔ cup*

Peel and chop one of the apples. Chop the onions and celery. Place in a large ovenproof dish with two-thirds of the butter and cook for 5 minutes on MICROWAVE HIGH.

Clean the pheasant well and stuff each with a peeled apple. Dredge the birds with some of the flour. Place, breast side down, on top of the softened vegetables. Cook for 5 minutes on COMBINATION HIGH 250°C. Turn the birds breast side up and cook for 5 minutes on COMBINATION HIGH 250°C. Remove the pheasants from the dish.

Stir one spoonful of the remaining flour into the vegetables. Slowly add the stock and cider, mixing constantly. Season to taste. Bury the bouquet garni amongst the vegetables and return the pheasant to the pan. Cover and cook for 40 minutes on COMBINATION MEDIUM 200°C. (Cooking time may vary slightly according to the size of the birds.)

While the pheasant are cooking, slice the remaining apple and sauté in the remaining butter until golden.

Remove the pheasant from the dish, carve and arrange on an attractive serving dish with the sautéed apple. Strain the sauce, stir in the cream and adjust the seasoning. Heat for 1 minute on MICROWAVE HIGH. Spoon some of the sauce over the pheasant and pass the remainder separately.

Coconut Chicken with Kidney Beans

Preparation time
15 minutes

Cooking time
10 minutes

To serve 4

Ingredients	Metric	Imperial	American
Onion	*1*	*1*	*1*
Garlic	*2 cloves*	*2 cloves*	*2 cloves*
Fresh green chillis	*1–2*	*1–2*	*1–2*
Oil	*30 ml*	*2 tbsp*	*2 tbsp*
Cooked chicken	*450 g*	*1 lb*	*1 lb*
Cooked ham	*50 g*	*2 oz*	*2 oz*
Cooked kidney beans	*225 g*	*8 oz*	*½ lb*
Creamed coconut or	*50 g*	*2 oz*	*¼ cup*
coconut milk	*50 ml*	*2 fl oz*	*¼ cup*

Peel the onion, cut in half and slice thinly. Peel and chop the garlic. Seed and slice the chillis. If you like hot food, leave a few of the seeds in the chilli. Place in a large casserole, cover and soften for 5 minutes on MICROWAVE HIGH.

Dice the chicken and ham. Add to the vegetables along with the kidney beans. Add the creamed coconut or coconut milk and cook for 5 minutes on COMBINATION HIGH 250°C. Serve with rice.

Lemon and Thyme Chicken

Preparation time
5 minutes plus 6 hours marinating time

Cooking time
20–30 minutes

To serve 4

Ingredients	Metric	Imperial	American
Chicken portions	*4*	*4*	*4*
Salt and pepper			
Large lemon	*1*	*1*	*1*
Sprigs fresh thyme	*8*	*8*	*8*
or dried thyme	*5 ml*	*1 tsp*	*1 tsp*
Garlic	*1 clove*	*1 clove*	*1 clove*
Olive oil	*60 ml*	*4 tbsp*	*4 tbsp*

Place the chicken portions in a well greased shallow baking dish. Season to taste with salt and pepper.

Finely grate the rind of the lemon and mix with the juice. Add chopped thyme and crushed garlic then whisk in the olive oil. Pour over the chicken and leave to marinate for at least 6 hours, turning occasionally.

Bake the chicken for 20 – 30 minutes on COMBINATION HIGH 250°C, basting frequently with the marinade.

Turkey and Broccoli Lasagne

Preparation time
15 minutes

Cooking time
35 minutes

To serve 4

Ingredients	Metric	Imperial	American
Lasagne noodles	*225 g*	*8 oz*	*½ lb*
Broccoli	*225 g*	*8 oz*	*½ lb*
Margarine	*30 ml*	*2 tbsp*	*2 tbsp*
Flour	*30 ml*	*2 tbsp*	*2 tbsp*
Milk	*300 ml*	*½ pint*	*1¼ cups*
Grated Emmenthal cheese	*125 g*	*4 oz*	*½ cup*
Salt and pepper			
Turkey steaks (raw)	*225 g*	*8 oz*	*½ lb*
Butter or margarine	*50 g*	*2 oz*	*2 oz*
Tomato sauce (Passata)	*250 ml*	*8 fl oz*	*1 cup*
Sugar	*pinch*	*pinch*	*pinch*
Dried basil	*pinch*	*pinch*	*pinch*
Dried oregano	*pinch*	*pinch*	*pinch*
Mozzarella cheese	*125 g*	*4 oz*	*4 oz*
Parmesan cheese, grated	*30 ml*	*2 tbsp*	*2 tbsp*

Cook the lasagne noodles in the usual way, drain and spread in a single layer on a clean tea towel to cool.

Cook the broccoli with a few spoonsful of water in a covered dish for 10 minutes on MICROWAVE HIGH. Drain, chop and set aside.

Place the margarine in a jug and melt on MICROWAVE HIGH. Stir in the flour and gradually add the milk, stirring constantly. Cook for 5 minutes on MICROWAVE HIGH, stirring once halfway through. Whisk until smooth, stir in the Emmenthal and mix well. Season to taste.

Place the turkey steaks in a shallow dish. Dot with the butter or margarine and cook for 10 minutes on COMBINATION HIGH 250°C. Cool then cut into thin slivers.

Combine the tomato sauce, sugar, basil and oregano. Spread a few spoonsful of sauce over the bottom of a shallow ovenproof dish. Arrange a layer of noodles over the sauce then sprinkle with broccoli, turkey and sliced Mozzarella. Sprinkle with a few spoonsful of tomato sauce. Repeat these layers ending with noodles. Top with cheese sauce and sprinkle with Parmesan. Bake for 10 minutes on COMBINATION HIGH 250°C to heat and brown.

Note: the turkey can be replaced with chicken or fish, the broccoli can be replaced with leeks, cauliflower or spinach. For a more traditional Italian lasagne, brown minced beef with an onion and omit the vegetables.

Venison with Orange

Preparation time
15 minutes

Cooking time
30 minutes

To serve 4

Ingredients	Metric	Imperial	American
Venison	*675 g*	*1½ lb*	*1½ lb*
Orange	*1*	*1*	*1*
Red wine	*50 ml*	*2 fl oz*	*¼ cup*
Cloves	*4*	*4*	*4*
Double (heavy) cream	*50 ml*	*2 fl oz*	*¼ cup*

Cut the venison into bite-sized cubes. Place in a large casserole with the juice and grated rind of the orange. Pour over the wine which should be Portuguese for preference. Add the cloves, cover and cook for 30 minutes on COMBINATION LOW 220°C.

Stir the cream into the casserole just before serving.

Coriander Chicken

Preparation time
10 minutes

Cooking time
50 minutes

To serve 4

Ingredients	Metric	Imperial	American
Chicken	*1 (1½ kg)*	*1 (3½ lb)*	*1 (3½ lb)*
Tomatoes	*225 g*	*8 oz*	*½ lb*
Garlic	*1 clove*	*1 clove*	*1 clove*
Onion	*1*	*1*	*1*
Cinnamon stick	*1*	*1*	*1*
Cumin seeds	*5 ml*	*1 tsp*	*1 tsp*
Chopped fresh coriander	*15 ml*	*1 tbsp*	*1 tbsp*
Cooked red kidney beans	*225 g*	*8 oz*	*½ lb*
Cooked chick peas	*225 g*	*8 oz*	*½ lb*
Salt	*2½ ml*	*½ tsp*	*½ tsp*

Cut the chicken into quarters and arrange in a single layer in a large casserole.

Peel and chop the tomatoes or use tomato sauce for a smoother sauce. Add to the chicken along with the chopped garlic, sliced onion, cinnamon stick, cumin seeds and coriander. Cover the casserole and cook for 30 minutes on COMBINATION HIGH 250°C. Uncover the casserole and cook for a further 15 minutes on COMBINATION HIGH 250°C.

Add the kidney beans and chick peas to the casserole, mix well and cook for 5 minutes on MICROWAVE HIGH. Add salt and mix well.

Chicken with Peppers

Preparation time
10 minutes

Cooking time
45 minutes

To serve 4

Ingredients	Metric	Imperial	American
Red pepper	*½*	*½*	*½*
Green pepper	*½*	*½*	*½*
Mushrooms	*125 g*	*4 oz*	*¼ lb*
Oil	*30 ml*	*2 tbsp*	*2 tbsp*
Chicken	*1 (1½ kg)*	*1 (3½ lb)*	*1 (3½ lb)*
Dried rosemary	*pinch*	*pinch*	*pinch*
White wine	*125 ml*	*4 fl oz*	*½ cup*

Thinly slice the peppers and mushrooms. Place in a large, ovenproof dish and sprinkle with oil. Cover and soften for 5 minutes on MICROWAVE HIGH.

Place the chicken, breast side down, on top of the bed of vegetables. Sprinkle with rosemary and pour over the wine and roast for 40 minutes on COMBINATION HIGH 250°C. Turn breast side up halfway through the cooking time.

Alternatively, the chicken can be cut in half or quarters and cooked for 20 minutes only.

Chicken and Red Wine Casserole

Preparation time
15 minutes

Cooking time
40 minutes

To serve 4

Ingredients	Metric	Imperial	American
Streaky bacon	*4 rashers*	*4 rashers*	*4 rashers*
Turnips	*4*	*4*	*4*
Tomatoes	*4*	*4*	*4*
Carrots	*4*	*4*	*4*
Onion	*1*	*1*	*1*
Chicken	*1 (1½ kg)*	*1 (3½ lb)*	*1 (3½ lb)*
Red wine	*250 ml*	*8 fl oz*	*1 cup*

Dice the bacon and place in a large shallow casserole. Peel the vegetables and cut into large chunks. Add to the casserole.

Cut the chicken into serving pieces and arrange, skin side up, in a single layer in the casserole. Pour over the wine, cover and cook for 30 minutes on COMBINATION HIGH 250°C. Remove the lid and cook for a further 5 minutes on COMBINATION HIGH 250°C. To make the casserole more substantial, a drained can of red kidney beans can be added during the last 5 minutes of cooking time.

CAKES AND DESSERTS

Baked desserts illustrate the benefits of combination cooking. The results are indistinguishable from conventionally baked items but are cooked in a fraction of the time. Cakes, too, cook quickly and the results are delicious.

Fruit Crumb Pie (page 85); Cherry Almond Cake (page 93); Streusel Coffee Cake (page 96).

Buttered Apples

Preparation time
10 minutes

Cooking time
10 minutes

To serve 4

Ingredients	Metric	Imperial	American
Apples	*450 g*	*1 lb*	*1 lb*
Unsalted butter	*45 ml*	*3 tbsp*	*3 tbsp*
Sugar	*5 ml*	*1 tsp*	*1 tsp*

Peel, core and thinly slice the apples.

Melt the butter on MICROWAVE HIGH. Toss the apples in butter, sprinkle with sugar, cover and cook for 10 minutes on COMBINATION HIGH 250°C. Serve the apples either as a dessert or as an accompaniment to roast pork.

Gooseberry Pudding

Preparation time
25 minutes

Cooking time
30 minutes

To serve 6–8

Ingredients	Metric	Imperial	American
Topping			
Butter	*30 ml*	*2 tbsp*	*2 tsp*
Golden sugar	*60 ml*	*4 tbsp*	*4 tbsp*
Pudding			
Gooseberries	*450 g*	*1 lb*	*1 lb*
Butter	*125 g*	*4 oz*	*½ cup*
Eggs	*2*	*2*	*2*
Sugar	*175 g*	*6 oz*	*¾ cup*
Plain (all-purpose) flour	*125 g*	*4 oz*	*1 cup*
Gin	*30 ml*	*2 tbsp*	*2 tbsp*

Melt the butter and golden sugar for the topping in a 1.15 litre/2 pint casserole for 2 minutes on MICROWAVE HIGH.

Wash and top and tail the gooseberries. Pack them tightly into the casserole.

Melt the butter for the pudding on MICROWAVE HIGH.

Whisk the eggs and sugar until they are light and frothy. Fold in the flour, gin and melted butter. Mix well and pour over the gooseberries. Bake on the rack in the oven for 25 minutes at COMBINATION MEDIUM 220°C. Turn out pudding to serve.

If you are using a combination oven without a fan, it will be necessary to preheat the oven for 10 minutes before baking the pudding.

Fruit Crumb Pie

Preparation time
20 minutes

Cooking time
15 minutes

To serve 4–6

Ingredients	Metric	Imperial	American
Pastry			
Plain (pastry) flour	*175 g*	*6 oz*	*1½ cups*
Baking powder	*4 ml*	*¾ tsp*	*¾ tsp*
Salt	*pinch*	*pinch*	*pinch*
Sugar	*30 ml*	*2 tbsp*	*2 tbsp*
Margarine	*125 g*	*4 oz*	*½ cup*
Egg	*1*	*1*	*1*
Filling			
Fruit (see below)	*900 g*	*2 lb*	*2 lb*
Sugar	*50 g*	*2 oz*	*¼ cup*
Cornflour (cornstarch)	*5 ml*	*1 tsp*	*1 tsp*
Cinnamon	*2½ ml*	*½ tsp*	*½ tsp*
Water	*30 ml*	*2 tbsp*	*2 tbsp*
Topping			
Plain (pastry) flour	*125 g*	*4 oz*	*1 cup*
Butter	*50 g*	*2 oz*	*¼ cup*
Sugar	*30 ml*	*2 tbsp*	*2 tbsp*

Combine the dry ingredients for the pastry. Rub in the margarine until the mixture resembles coarse breadcrumbs. Bind with beaten egg and press gently over the base and sides of a glass pie dish.

Prepare the fruit for the filling according to type. Berries, peaches, apples, plums etc. are all delicious. Combine the dry ingredients, sprinkle over the fruit and toss to coat. Sprinkle with water and turn into the pastry-lined pie dish.

Rub together the flour and butter for the topping until the mixture resembles coarse breadcrumbs. Gently mix in the sugar. Spread evenly over the fruit and bake for 15 minutes on COMBINATION HIGH 220°C. Cool and sprinkle generously with sieved icing (confectioners') sugar before serving.

If you are using a combination oven without a fan, it will be necessary to preheat the oven for 10 minutes before baking the pie.

Caramel Apple Pie

Preparation time
25 minutes

Cooking time
16 minutes plus 10 minutes resting time

To serve 4–6

Ingredients	Metric	Imperial	American
Caramel			
Light brown sugar	*175 g*	*6 oz*	*¾ cup*
Unsalted butter	*30 ml*	*2 tbsp*	*2 tbsp*
Water	*30 ml*	*2 tbsp*	*2 tbsp*
Filling			
Apples	*450 g*	*1 lb*	*1 lb*
Pastry			
Plain (pastry) flour	*225 g*	*8 oz*	*2 cups*
Mixed spice	*pinch*	*pinch*	*pinch*
Dark brown sugar	*30 ml*	*2 tbsp*	*2 tbsp*
Margarine	*125 g*	*4 oz*	*½ cup*
Oil	*15 ml*	*1 tbsp*	*1 tbsp*
Egg	*1*	*1*	*1*

Place the caramel ingredients in a glass pie dish and cook for 6 minutes on MICROWAVE HIGH to make the caramel. Tip the dish to ensure the base is completely coated.

Peel, core and slice the apples. Arrange in overlapping rings in the base of the pie dish.

Combine the dry ingredients for the pastry. Rub in the margarine until the mixture resembles coarse breadcrumbs. Beat the eggs, mix with the oil and stir into the flour mixture until a dough is formed. Roll out to make a round approximately ½ cm/¼ inch thick and place over the apples. Bake the pie for 10 minutes on COMBINATION HIGH 220°C. Rest for 10 minutes then turn out onto a serving dish so that the caramelised apples sit on top of their pastry base.

If you are using a combination oven without a fan, it will be necessary to preheat the oven for 10 minutes before baking the pie.

Rice Pudding

Preparation time
5 minutes

Cooking time
45 minutes

To serve 4

Ingredients	Metric	Imperial	American
Long grain rice	*45 ml*	*3 tbsp*	*3 tbsp*
Sugar	*15 ml*	*1 tbsp*	*1 tbsp*
Sultanas (golden raisins)	*30 ml*	*2 tbsp*	*2 tbsp*
Milk	*575 ml*	*1 pint*	*2½ cups*
Ground nutmeg	*pinch*	*pinch*	*pinch*

Place the rice, sugar and sultanas in a large ovenproof dish. Mix well, add milk and sprinkle with nutmeg. Bake for 45 minutes on COMBINATION LOW 160°C.

The sultanas can be replaced with dried apricots, mixed peel, dates or whatever else is available to provide variety.

Gingered Peaches

Preparation time
10 minutes

Cooking time
5 minutes

To serve 4

Ingredients	Metric	Imperial	American
Peach halves (fresh or canned)	*8*	*8*	*8*
Stem ginger	*1 knob*	*1 knob*	*1 knob*
Golden or demerara sugar	*40 ml*	*8 tsp*	*8 tsp*
Unsalted butter	*30 ml*	*2 tbsp*	*2 tbsp*

Arrange the peach halves in a single layer in a greased ovenproof dish, hollows uppermost. If using fresh peaches, plunge into boiling water for 1 minute then remove, peel away skin and cut the peaches in half. Remove the stone.

Dice the stem ginger and divide evenly between the eight peach halves. Sprinkle with sugar and top with a dot of butter. Bake the peaches for 5 minutes on COMBINATION HIGH 200°C.

Gingered peaches make a delicious accompaniment to roast pork or can be served, with fresh cream or ice cream, as dessert.

Pumpkin Pie

Preparation time
20 minutes plus 1 hour chilling time

Cooking time
30 minutes plus cooling time

To serve 8–10

Ingredients	Metric	Imperial	American
Pastry			
Butter	*50 g*	*2 oz*	*¼ cup*
Margarine	*50 g*	*2 oz*	*¼ cup*
Plain (pastry) flour	*175 g*	*6 oz*	*1½ cups*
Egg	*1*	*1*	*1*
Filling			
Pumpkin purée	*450 g*	*1 lb*	*2 cups*
Eggs	*2*	*2*	*2*
Sugar	*225 g*	*8 oz*	*1 cup*
Ground cinnamon	*5 ml*	*1 tsp*	*1 tsp*
Ground cloves	*2½ ml*	*½ tsp*	*½ tsp*
Ground nutmeg	*2½ ml*	*½ tsp*	*½ tsp*
Ground ginger	*2½ ml*	*½ tsp*	*½ tsp*
Salt	*pinch*	*pinch*	*pinch*
Evaporated milk	*410 ml*	*14½ fl oz*	*1¾ cups*

To prepare the pastry, rub the butter and margarine into the flour until the mixture resembles coarse breadcrumbs. Bind to a dough with the beaten egg. If necessary, add a few drops of water. Wrap in clingfilm and chill for 1 hour.

Beat the pumpkin purée with the eggs until smooth. Combine the sugar, spices and salt. Add to the purée and mix well. Stir in the evaporated milk.

Roll out the dough to line the base and sides of a 23 cm/ 9 inch diameter deep pie dish. Carefully pour in the filling mixture. Bake the pie for 30 minutes on COMBINATION LOW 250°C. Leave to cool before serving with whipped or pouring cream.

If you are using a combination oven without a fan, it will be necessary to preheat the oven for 10 minutes before baking the pie.

Note: pumpkin pie goes particularly well with pecans. When the pie is half baked and the filling just beginning to set, arrange pecan halves in a decorative pattern on top.

Bourbon Bread Pudding

Preparation time
15 minutes plus 1 hour resting time

Cooking time
20 minutes

To serve 4

Ingredients	Metric	Imperial	American
Sultanas (golden raisins)	*30 ml*	*2 tbsp*	*2 tbsp*
Raisins	*30 ml*	*2 tbsp*	*2 tbsp*
Bourbon	*90 ml*	*6 tbsp*	*6 tbsp*
White bread	*6 slices*	*6 slices*	*6 slices*
Butter	*30 ml*	*2 tbsp*	*2 tbsp*
Cinnamon	*5 ml*	*1 tsp*	*1 tsp*
Ground nutmeg	*2½ ml*	*½ tsp*	*½ tsp*
Ground cloves	*2½ ml*	*½ tsp*	*½ tsp*
Ground ginger	*2½ ml*	*½ tsp*	*½ tsp*
Eggs	*2*	*2*	*2*
Milk	*250 ml*	*8 fl oz*	*1 cup*
Single (light) cream	*250 ml*	*8 fl oz*	*1 cup*
Caster sugar	*30 ml*	*2 tbsp*	*2 tbsp*
Demerara or golden sugar	*15 ml*	*1 tbsp*	*1 tbsp*

Soak the sultanas and raisins in bourbon for 30 minutes. Rum or any other spirit you prefer can be substituted for bourbon.

Remove the crusts from the bread, spread bread with butter and cut into fingers.

Combine the spices, eggs, milk, cream and caster sugar. Mix well. Drain the sultanas and raisins. Add the bourbon to the egg mixture.

Place a layer of bread in a greased ovenproof dish. Sprinkle with fruit. Repeat the layers, until there is none left, ending with bread. Pour over the egg mixture and leave for 30 minutes.

Sprinkle demerara or golden sugar over the top of the pudding and bake for 20 minutes on COMBINATION LOW 200°C.

If you are using a combination oven without a fan, it will be necessary to preheat the oven for 10 minutes before baking the pudding.

Baked Raisin Pudding

Preparation time
5 minutes plus 10 minutes resting time

Cooking time
15 minutes

To serve 4

Ingredients	Metric	Imperial	American
Raisins	*225 g*	*8 oz*	*1 cup*
Rum	*125 ml*	*4 fl oz*	*½ cup*
Milk	*300 ml*	*½ pint*	*1¼ cups*
Plain (all-purpose) flour	*125 g*	*4 oz*	*1 cup*
Sugar	*150 g*	*5 oz*	*⅔ cup*
Eggs	*2*	*2*	*2*
Unsalted butter	*30 ml*	*2 tbsp*	*2 tbsp*

Soak the raisins in the rum for 10 minutes. Scald the milk on MICROWAVE HIGH.

Combine the flour, sugar, milk and eggs to make a batter. Mix well.

Add the rum and raisins to the batter and fold in gently.

Thickly spread the butter over the base and sides of a 20 cm/8 inch glass flan or pie dish. Pour the batter into the dish and bake for 15 minutes on COMBINATION HIGH 250°C.

If you are using a combination oven without a fan, it will be necessary to preheat the oven for 10 minutes before baking the pudding.

Baked Bananas

Preparation time
5 minutes

Cooking time
5 minutes

To serve 4

Ingredients	Metric	Imperial	American
Bananas	*4*	*4*	*4*
Rum	*60 ml*	*4 tbsp*	*4 tbsp*
Butter	*20 ml*	*4 tsp*	*4 tsp*
Brown sugar	*20 ml*	*4 tsp*	*4 tsp*
Lime juice	*20 ml*	*4 tsp*	*4 tsp*
Mixed spice	*pinch*	*pinch*	*pinch*

Peel the bananas and slice in half lengthways. Arrange in a single layer in a greased shallow ovenproof dish. Pour over the rum and dot with butter. Sprinkle with sugar, lime juice and mixed spice. Bake the bananas for 5 minutes on COMBINATION HIGH 200°C. Serve hot with double cream, ice cream or your favourite light sorbet.

Note: pineapple rings can be cooked in the same way and Kirsch substituted for the rum.

Cherry Almond Cake

Preparation time
20 minutes

Cooking time
15 minutes

Makes 1

Ingredients	Metric	Imperial	American
Margarine	*75 g*	*3 oz*	*1/3 cup*
Sugar	*175 g*	*6 oz*	*3/4 cup*
Eggs	*2*	*2*	*2*
Plain (all-purpose) flour	*200 g*	*7 oz*	*1 3/4 cups*
Baking powder	*10 ml*	*2 tsp*	*2 tsp*
Salt	*2 1/2 ml*	*1/2 tsp*	*1/2 tsp*
Milk	*125 ml*	*4 fl oz*	*1/2 cup*
Almond essence (extract)	*2 1/2 ml*	*1/2 tsp*	*1/2 tsp*
Glacé cherries	*125 g*	*4 oz*	*1/2 cup*

Cream the margarine and sugar until light and fluffy. Add the eggs, one at a time, beating well after each.

Sieve together the flour and baking powder. Stir in the salt. Combine the milk and almond essence.

Add the flour mixture and milk alternately to the egg mixture, folding in gently.

Rinse the cherries and dice. Stir into the cake batter.

Grease a 1.15 litre/2 pint soufflé or deep cake dish, line with greaseproof paper and pour in the batter. Bake for 15 minutes on COMBINATION MEDIUM 250°C. Alternatively, pour the batter into two greased and lined 450 g/1 lb loaf dishes and bake as before.

If you are using a combination oven without a fan, it will be necessary to preheat the oven for 10 minutes before baking the cake.

The cake can be served as it is or filled and frosted with almond flavoured butter icing then decorated with sliced cherries.

Note: to make a coffee walnut cake, substitute coffee essence (extract) and chopped walnuts for almond essence (extract) and glacé cherries.

Tea Time Spongecake

Preparation time
20 minutes

Cooking time
13 minutes

Makes 1

Ingredients	Metric	Imperial	American
Eggs	*4*	*4*	*4*
Caster sugar	*125 g*	*4 oz*	*½ cup*
Self-raising flour	*125 g*	*4 oz*	*1 cup*
Filling			
Jam	*45 ml*	*3 tbsp*	*3 tbsp*
Brandy	*5 ml*	*1 tsp*	*1 tsp*
Double (heavy) cream	*150 ml*	*¼ pint*	*⅔ cup*

Whisk the eggs and sugar together until very thick and almost white. If you do not have an electric mixer, this should be done over a bowl of warm water.

Gently fold in the sieved flour. Turn into two greased and lined glass sandwich pans. Place one pan directly on the turntable and the other on the rack. Bake for 10 minutes on COMBINATION LOW 250°C then remove the top layer and rack and continue baking the second layer for a further 2 minutes.

If you are using a combination oven without a fan, it will be necessary to preheat the oven for 10 minutes before baking the cake.

Warm the jam for 1 minute on MICROWAVE MEDIUM. Stir in the brandy and spread evenly over one layer of spongecake.

Whisk the cream until it is firm and spread over the jam. Rest the top layer of sponge on top of the cream.

Note: to make a chocolate sponge, substitute equal amounts of cornflour (cornstarch) and cocoa powder for the self-raising flour. The whipped cream can be flavoured with 125 g/4 oz of melted chocolate and the jam replaced by a brandy flavoured sugar syrup.

Streusel Coffee Cake

Preparation time
15 minutes

Cooking time
12 minutes

Makes 1

Ingredients	Metric	Imperial	American
Margarine	*50 g*	*2 oz*	*¼ cup*
Sugar	*125 g*	*4 oz*	*½ cup*
Egg	*1*	*1*	*1*
Vanilla essence (extract)	*2½ ml*	*½ tsp*	*½ tsp*
Coffee essence (extract)	*10 ml*	*2 tsp*	*2 tsp*
Self-raising flour	*125 g*	*4 oz*	*1 cup*
Salt	*2½ ml*	*½ tsp*	*½ tsp*
Milk	*50 ml*	*2 fl oz*	*¼ cup*
Raisins	*50 g*	*2 oz*	*¼ cup*
Streusel topping			
Plain (pastry) flour	*30 ml*	*2 tbsp*	*2 tbsp*
Brown sugar	*75 g*	*3 oz*	*⅓ cup*
Cinnamon	*2½ ml*	*½ tsp*	*½ tsp*
Butter	*50 g*	*2 oz*	*¼ cup*
Chopped nuts	*50 g*	*2 oz*	*¼ cup*

Cream the margarine and sugar until light and fluffy. Add the egg and mix well. Stir in the vanilla and coffee essences.

Combine the flour and salt. Fold into the sugar mixture, alternating with the milk. Mix well. Stir in the raisins.

Combine the flour, sugar and cinnamon for the topping. Rub in the butter until the mixture resembles coarse crumbs. Stir in the chopped nuts — walnuts, hazelnuts, pecans or a mixture are all delicious.

Sprinkle half of the topping mixture over the base of a 1.15 litre/2 pint greased soufflé or cake dish. Spoon in the batter and sprinkle with the remaining topping. Bake the cake for 12 minutes on COMBINATION MEDIUM 250°C.

If you are using a combination oven without a fan, it will be necessary to preheat the oven for 10 minutes before baking the cake.

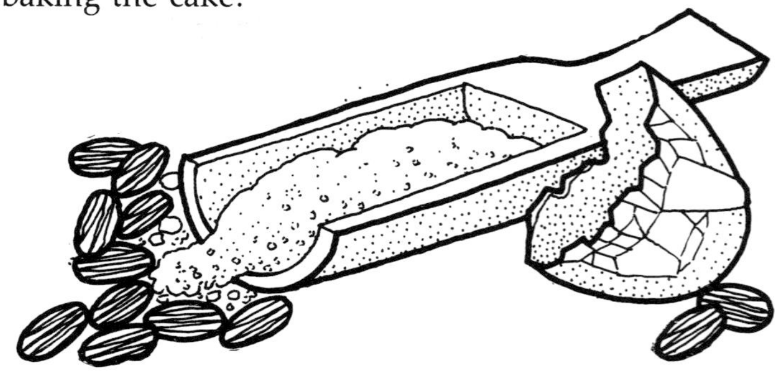

Chocolate Almond Cake

Preparation time
15 minutes

Cooking time
12 minutes

Makes 1

Ingredients	Metric	Imperial	American
Margarine	*125 g*	*4 oz*	*½ cup*
Sugar	*125 g*	*4 oz*	*½ cup*
Eggs	*2*	*2*	*2*
Almond essence (extract)	*2½ ml*	*½ tsp*	*½ tsp*
Self-raising flour	*125 g*	*4 oz*	*1 cup*
Baking powder	*2½ ml*	*½ tsp*	*½ tsp*
Cocoa powder	*20 g*	*¾ oz*	*¼ cup*
Ground almonds	*30 ml*	*2 tbsp*	*2 tbsp*
Milk	*50 ml*	*2 fl oz*	*¼ cup*

Cream the margarine and sugar until light and fluffy. Add the eggs, one at a time, beating well after each. Add the almond essence and mix well.

Sieve together the flour, baking powder and cocoa. Stir in the ground almonds.

Add the flour mixture and milk alternately to the egg mixture, folding in gently.

Grease a 1.15 litre/2 pint soufflé or deep cake dish, line with greased greaseproof paper and pour in the batter. Bake for 12 minutes on COMBINATION MEDIUM 200°C.

If you are using a combination oven without a fan, it will be necessary to preheat the oven for 10 minutes before baking the cake.

Family Chocolate Cake

Preparation time
15 minutes

Cooking time
15 minutes

Makes 1

Ingredients	Metric	Imperial	American
Margarine	*125 g*	*4 oz*	*½ cup*
Sugar	*175 g*	*6 oz*	*¾ cup*
Eggs	*2*	*2*	*2*
Vanilla essence (extract)	*5 ml*	*1 tsp*	*1 tsp*
Plain (all-purpose) flour	*200 g*	*7 oz*	*1¾ cups*
Baking powder	*7½ ml*	*1½ tsp*	*1½ tsp*
Bicarbonate of soda (baking soda)	*5 ml*	*1 tsp*	*1 tsp*
Salt	*pinch*	*pinch*	*pinch*
Cocoa powder	*40 g*	*1½ oz*	*¼ cup*
Water	*250 ml*	*8 fl oz*	*1 cup*

Cream the margarine and sugar until light and fluffy. Add the eggs, one at a time, beating well after each. Add the vanilla and mix well.

Sieve together the flour, baking powder, bicarbonate of soda, salt and cocoa.

Add the flour mixture and water alternately to the egg mixture, folding in gently.

Grease a 1.15 litre/2 pint soufflé or deep cake dish, line with greased greaseproof paper and pour in the batter. Bake for 15 minutes on COMBINATION MEDIUM 250°C. Alternatively, pour the batter into two greased and lined 450 g/1 lb loaf dishes and bake as before.

If you are using a combination oven without a fan, it will be necessary to preheat the oven for 10 minutes before baking the cake.

The cake can be served as it is or filled and frosted with chocolate butter icing then decorated with nuts or glacé cherries.

Note: for double chocolate cake, stir a few spoonsful of chocolate chips into the batter before baking. For a luxury dessert, cut the cake into two layers, sprinkle with Kirsch then spread black cherry jam and whipped cream between the layers.

Feuilleté

Preparation time
15 minutes

Cooking time
5 minutes

To serve 4

Ingredients	Metric	Imperial	American
Puff pastry	*225 g*	*8 oz*	*½ lb*
Fruit (see below)	*125 g*	*4 oz*	*¼ lb*
Double (heavy) cream	*125 ml*	*4 fl oz*	*½ cup*
Icing (confectioners') sugar	*60 ml*	*4 tbsp*	*4 tbsp*
Water			
Red food colouring			

Roll out the pastry to make a rectangle. Place on a flat ovenproof dish and bake for 5 minutes on COMBINATION MEDIUM 250°C. Leave to cool.

Rinse, drain or defrost the fruit. Summer berries are especially delicious, but peaches, apricots or any other soft fruit can be used.

Whisk the cream until it is just firm enough to hold its shape.

Assemble the Feuilleté just before you are ready to serve it. Carefully cut the pastry in half through the centre to make two layers. Arrange the cream and fruit on the bottom layer and cover with the top layer.

Mix the sieved icing (confectioners') sugar with just enough water to make a thick paste. Set aside one spoonful and spread the remainder over the top of the pastry. Stir a few drops of food colouring into the reserved icing to make a pink paste. Fill an icing bag and pipe thin rows of pink icing over the length of the pastry. Using a skewer, carefully draw lines across the width of the pastry, dragging the icing to create a feathered effect. Serve immediately.

Rum and Ginger Cake

Preparation time
15 minutes

Cooking time
10 minutes

Makes 1

Ingredients	Metric	Imperial	American
Margarine	*50 g*	*2 oz*	*¼ cup*
Black treacle	*125 ml*	*4 fl oz*	*½ cup*
Egg	*1*	*1*	*1*
Rum	*50 ml*	*2 fl oz*	*¼ cup*
Self-raising flour	*125 g*	*4 oz*	*1 cup*
Ground ginger	*7½ ml*	*1½ tsp*	*1½ tsp*
Brown sugar	*75 g*	*3 oz*	*⅓ cup*
Stem ginger	*1 knob*	*1 knob*	*1 knob*

Melt the margarine and treacle on MICROWAVE HIGH.

Beat together the egg and rum. Add to the treacle along with the combined dry ingredients. Chop the stem ginger and stir into the batter which will be very soft.

Grease and line a 1.15 litre/2 pint soufflé dish. Grease a small ovenproof glass and place in the centre of the dish so that the cake is baked as a ring. Pour in the batter. Bake the cake for 10 minutes on COMBINATION MEDIUM 220°C. The mixture can also be poured into two greased and lined 450 g/1 lb loaf dishes and baked for the same time, but be sure that the dishes do not touch one another.

If you are using a combination oven without a fan, it will be necessary to preheat the oven for 10 minutes before baking the cake.

BREAD AND YEAST COOKING

There is nothing more homely than the aroma of homebaked bread and with a combination microwave you can cook bread and rolls quickly and well. Tea breads, made without yeast, can be prepared in a few minutes to delight unexpected guests.

Basic White Bread, Plait and Rolls (page 104); Fruit Crescent (page 108).

Basic White Bread

Preparation time
20 minutes plus proving time

Cooking time
15 minutes

Makes 2

Ingredients	Metric	Imperial	American
Strong (bread) flour	*675 g*	*1½ lb*	*6 cups*
Easy-blend yeast	*1 sachet*	*1 sachet*	*1 sachet*
Sugar	*5 ml*	*1 tsp*	*1 tsp*
Salt	*2½ ml*	*½ tsp*	*½ tsp*
Margarine	*50 g*	*2 oz*	*¼ cup*
Warm water or milk	*425 ml*	*¾ pint*	*2 cups*

Combine the flour, yeast, sugar and salt. (If you want to use conventional dried yeast or fresh yeast, reconstitute in the usual manner before adding to the flour.)

If you are using water, rub the margarine into the flour until the mixture resembles coarse crumbs. Add the water and mix to make a firm dough. Knead well until firm and elastic.

If you are using milk, heat it with the margarine for 1 minute on MICROWAVE HIGH. Add to the flour and mix to make a firm dough.

Turn the dough into a greased bowl, cover and leave to rise until it has doubled in bulk.

Punch down the risen dough, divide in half and roll out to make two large rectangles. Fold into thirds and press gently into two greased 450 g/1 lb glass loaf dishes or shape into a round, coil or plait as you like. Alternatively, make individual rolls and arrange with sides touching in a shallow round cake dish.

Cover the dough and leave to rise until it has doubled in bulk.

Brush the dough with milk and sprinkle with poppy or sesame seeds. Bake for 15 minutes on COMBINATION LOW 250°C.

If you are using a combination oven that does not have a fan, preheat the oven before baking the bread.

Note: cooking time may vary slightly depending on the shape you have chosen. This basic dough can be flavoured with mustard, grated cheese, onions, courgettes (zucchini) or herbs for variety.

Basic Brown Bread

Preparation time
20 minutes plus proving time

Cooking time
15 minutes

Makes 2

Ingredients	Metric	Imperial	American
Wholemeal or Granary flour	*675 g*	*1½ lb*	*6 cups*
Easy-blend yeast	*1 sachet*	*1 sachet*	*1 sachet*
Brown sugar	*5 ml*	*1 tsp*	*1 tsp*
Salt	*15 ml*	*1 tbsp*	*1 tbsp*
Vegetable fat	*50 g*	*2 oz*	*¼ cup*
Warm water	*425 ml*	*¾ pint*	*2 cups*

Combine the flour, yeast, sugar and salt. (If you want to use conventional dried yeast or fresh yeast, reconstitute in the usual manner before adding to the flour.)

Rub the fat into the flour until the mixture resembles coarse crumbs. Add the water and mix to make a firm dough. Knead well until firm and elastic.

Turn the dough into a greased bowl, cover and leave to rise until it has doubled in bulk.

Punch down the risen dough, divide in half and roll out to make two large rectangles. Fold into thirds and press gently into two greased 450 g/1 lb glass loaf dishes or shape into a round, coil or plait as you like. Alternatively, make individual rolls and arrange with sides touching in a round cake dish.

Cover the dough and leave to rise until it has doubled in bulk.

Bake the bread for 15 minutes on COMBINATION LOW 250°C. Brush with salt water when you remove the bread from the oven.

If you are using a combination oven that does not have a fan, preheat the oven before baking the bread.

Note: cooking time may vary slightly depending on the shape you have chosen. Before baking, the dough can be sprinkled with sesame seeds, wheatgerm or crushed cornflakes for extra texture. For a lighter loaf, replace half of the wholemeal flour with strong white flour. Rye flour can also be used with either half wholemeal or half white flour.

Cheese Buns

Preparation time
25 minutes plus proving time

Cooking time
15 minutes

Makes 12

Ingredients	Metric	Imperial	American
Milk	*175 ml*	*6 fl oz*	*¾ cup*
Butter	*30 ml*	*2 tbsp*	*2 tbsp*
Easy-blend yeast	*1 sachet*	*1 sachet*	*1 sachet*
Strong white (bread) flour	*675 g*	*1½ lb*	*6 cups*
Salt	*5 ml*	*1 tsp*	*1 tsp*
Dry mustard	*5 ml*	*1 tsp*	*1 tsp*
Warm water	*275 ml*	*8 fl oz*	*1 cup*
Grated Cheddar cheese	*125 g*	*4 oz*	*½ cup*
Chopped onion or celery	*50 g*	*2 oz*	*¼ cup*
Egg	*1*	*1*	*1*
Sesame or poppy seeds	*15 ml*	*1 tbsp*	*1 tbsp*

Heat the milk and butter for 1 minute on MICROWAVE HIGH.

Combine the yeast, flour, salt and mustard. (If you want to use conventional dried yeast or fresh yeast, reconstitute in the usual way before using.)

Stir the grated cheese and finely chopped onion or celery into the flour. Add the milk and butter and mix to form a dough. Gradually add water as necessary. Knead until the dough is firm and elastic. Place in a greased bowl, cover and leave to rise until it has doubled in bulk.

Punch down the dough and divide into sixteen pieces. Roll each one with your hands to make finger shapes. Place in a greased ovenproof dish, cover and leave to rise until doubled in bulk.

Whisk the egg and brush over the surface of the buns. Sprinkle with sesame or poppy seeds. Bake for 14 minutes on COMBINATION LOW 250°C.

If your oven does not have a fan, preheat before baking the bread.

Sourdough Bread

Preparation time
25 minutes plus time for making starter and proving time

Cooking time
15 minutes

Makes 2

Ingredients	Metric	Imperial	American
Starter			
Dried yeast	*5 ml*	*1 tsp*	*1 tsp*
Strong (bread) flour	*225 g*	*8 oz*	*2 cups*
Milk	*450 ml*	*15 fl. oz*	*2 cups*
Sugar	*125 g*	*4 oz*	*½ cup*
Bread			
Milk	*250 ml*	*8 fl oz*	*1 cup*
Margarine	*30 ml*	*2 tbsp*	*2 tbsp*
Strong (bread) flour	*675 g*	*1 ½ lb*	*6 cups*
Sugar	*15 ml*	*1 tbsp*	*1 tbsp*
Salt	*5 ml*	*1 tsp*	*1 tsp*
Easy-blend yeast	*1 pkg*	*1 pkg*	*1 pkg*
Starter (see above)	*350 ml*	*12 fl oz*	*1 ½ cups*

The sourdough starter needs 3–4 days to mature, but once started, can be topped up and kept indefinitely. Combine the dried yeast with half of each of flour, milk and sugar. Keep in an uncovered bowl in the kitchen and stir down two or three times a day. The remaining flour, milk and sugar should be added 8 hours before you are ready to use the starter.

To make Sourdough Bread: heat the milk and margarine for 1 minute on MICROWAVE HIGH or until the margarine has melted. Cool until lukewarm.

Combine the flour, sugar, salt and yeast. If you want to use conventional dried or fresh yeast, mix with some of the lukewarm milk and leave for 10 minutes until bubbly.

Add the milk and starter to the flour. Mix to make a stiff dough and knead until firm and elastic. Place in a greased bowl, cover and leave to rise until it has doubled in bulk, approximately 1 hour in a warm place.

Punch down the risen dough and divide in half. Shape each piece to fit into a greased glass loaf pan or make round loaves to bake in cake dishes. Cover and leave to rise again.

Bake the Sourdough Bread for 15 minutes on COMBINATION LOW 250°C. If you are using a combination oven that does not have a fan, preheat the oven before baking.

Note: cooking time may vary slightly depending on the shape. Wholewheat or rye flour can be substituted for half the strong white flour when making the bread dough.

Fruit Crescent

Preparation time
25 minutes plus proving time

Cooking time
20 minutes

Makes 2

Ingredients	Metric	Imperial	American
Dough			
Strong (bread) flour	*675 g*	*1½ lb*	*6 cups*
Easy-blend yeast	*1 sachet*	*1 sachet*	*1 sachet*
Sugar	*5 ml*	*1 tsp*	*1 tsp*
Salt	*2½ ml*	*½ tsp*	*½ tsp*
Milk	*300 ml*	*½ pint*	*1¼ cups*
Margarine	*50 g*	*2 oz*	*¼ cup*
Filling			
Softened butter	*125 g*	*4 oz*	*½ cup*
Chopped pecans	*50 g*	*2 oz*	*¼ cup*
Raisins	*60 ml*	*4 tbsp*	*4 tbsp*
Glacé cherries	*60 ml*	*4 tbsp*	*4 tbsp*
Mixed peel	*15 ml*	*1 tbsp*	*1 tbsp*
Topping			
Icing (confectioners') sugar	*90 ml*	*6 tbsp*	*6 tbsp*
Water			

Combine the flour, yeast, sugar and salt. (Or reconstitute dried or fresh yeast as usual.)

Warm the milk and margarine for 1 minute on MICROWAVE HIGH. Add to the flour and mix to make a firm dough. Knead well. Turn into a greased bowl, cover and leave to rise until it has doubled in bulk.

Punch down the risen dough and roll out half the dough to make a large rectangle. Spread with a quarter of the butter. Fold the dough in thirds and gently seal the edges. Turn it a quarter turn so that a sealed edge faces you and carefully roll out again. Spread with another quarter of the butter, fold and seal. Repeat with remaining dough and butter. Cover and leave to rise for 30 minutes.

Roll out each portion of dough again to make large rectangles. Sprinkle each with chopped nuts, raisins, cherries and mixed peel. Roll up as for a Swiss roll and gently seal the ends. Place on a baking dish curving to form a crescent. Cover and leave to rise for 30 minutes. Bake the Fruit Crescents one at a time for 20 minutes on COMBINATION LOW 200°C. Cool.

If you are using a combination oven that does not have a fan, preheat the oven before baking the crescents.

Combine the sieved icing sugar with just enough water to make a thick paste. Spread over the cooled Fruit Crescents and garnish with nuts and cherries.

Banana Teabread

Preparation time
20 minutes

Cooking time
12 minutes

Makes 2

Ingredients	Metric	Imperial	American
Soft margarine	*125 g*	*4 oz*	*½ cup*
Brown sugar	*150 g*	*5 oz*	*⅔ cup*
Eggs	*2*	*2*	*2*
Mashed bananas	*225 g*	*8 oz*	*1 cup*
Self-raising flour	*225 g*	*8 oz*	*2 cups*
Salt	*pinch*	*pinch*	*pinch*
Chopped walnuts	*50 g*	*2 oz*	*¼ cup*

Cream the margarine and sugar until light and fluffy.

Beat the eggs and add to the sugar mixture a little bit at a time, mixing well. Fold in the remaining ingredients. Turn into two greased and lined 450 g/1 lb glass loaf dishes. Bake for 12 minutes on COMBINATION MEDIUM 220°C. Cool and wrap in foil. Serve sliced with butter.

If you are using a combination oven that does not have a fan, preheat the oven before baking the bread.

Cornbread

Preparation time
10 minutes

Cooking time
12 minutes

Makes 1

Ingredients	Metric	Imperial	American
Cornmeal	*175 g*	*6 oz*	*1½ cups*
Plain (all-purpose) flour	*75 g*	*3 oz*	*¾ cup*
Baking powder	*15 ml*	*1 tbsp*	*1 tbsp*
Salt	*2½ ml*	*½ tsp*	*½ tsp*
Sugar	*30 ml*	*2 tbsp*	*2 tbsp*
Margarine	*50 g*	*2 oz*	*¼ cup*
Egg	*1*	*1*	*1*
Milk	*250 ml*	*8 fl oz*	*1 cup*

Combine the dry ingredients.

Melt the margarine on MICROWAVE HIGH then mix into the beaten egg and milk. Stir into the dry ingredients until just blended. The batter will be lumpy. Turn into a greased square or rectangular baking dish and bake for 12 minutes on COMBINATION MEDIUM 250°C. Serve hot or cold, in squares or slices, buttered or with jam; or as an accompaniment to fried chicken and gravy.

If you are using a combination oven that does not have a fan, preheat the oven before baking the bread.

Note: oil or melted bacon fat can be used instead of margarine and bits of crispy bacon added to the batter before baking. Crumbled cornbread can also be added to a bread stuffing for poultry.

INDEX

ATTACK
DA
BRONX
BOMBER

URBAN ART LEGENDS

KET

LOM ART

First published in Great Britain in 2015 by LOM Art, an imprint of
Michael O'Mara Books Limited
9 Lion Yard
Tremadoc Road
London SW4 7NQ

A CIP catalogue record for this book is available from the British Library.

Papers used by Michael O'Mara Books Limited are natural, recyclable products made from wood grown in sustainable forests. The manufacturing processes conform to the environmental regulations of the country of origin.

ISBN: 978-1-91055-205-6 in hardback print format

1 2 3 4 5 6 7 8 9 10

www.mombooks.com

Cover design by Jamie Keenan
Front cover image © Paul Green 2015 /
www.paulgreenphotography.com and courtesy of Nick Walker
Back cover, clockwise from top left, images courtesy of Banksy (photography by KET), JON ONE, Cost, Roa (photography by KET), Lady Pink, Doze Green, Risk, Daze, Slick and Drax
Designed and typeset by Ana Bjezancevic

Printed and bound in Malaysia

Above: Ray Staten, REVS, *Use the System Against the System*, New York, USA, 2013. Image courtesy of artist.
Following page: Daze, *Transition*, acrylic on canvas, 122 x 74 c.m., 1982. Museum of the City of New York / Martin Wong Collection.

CONTENTS

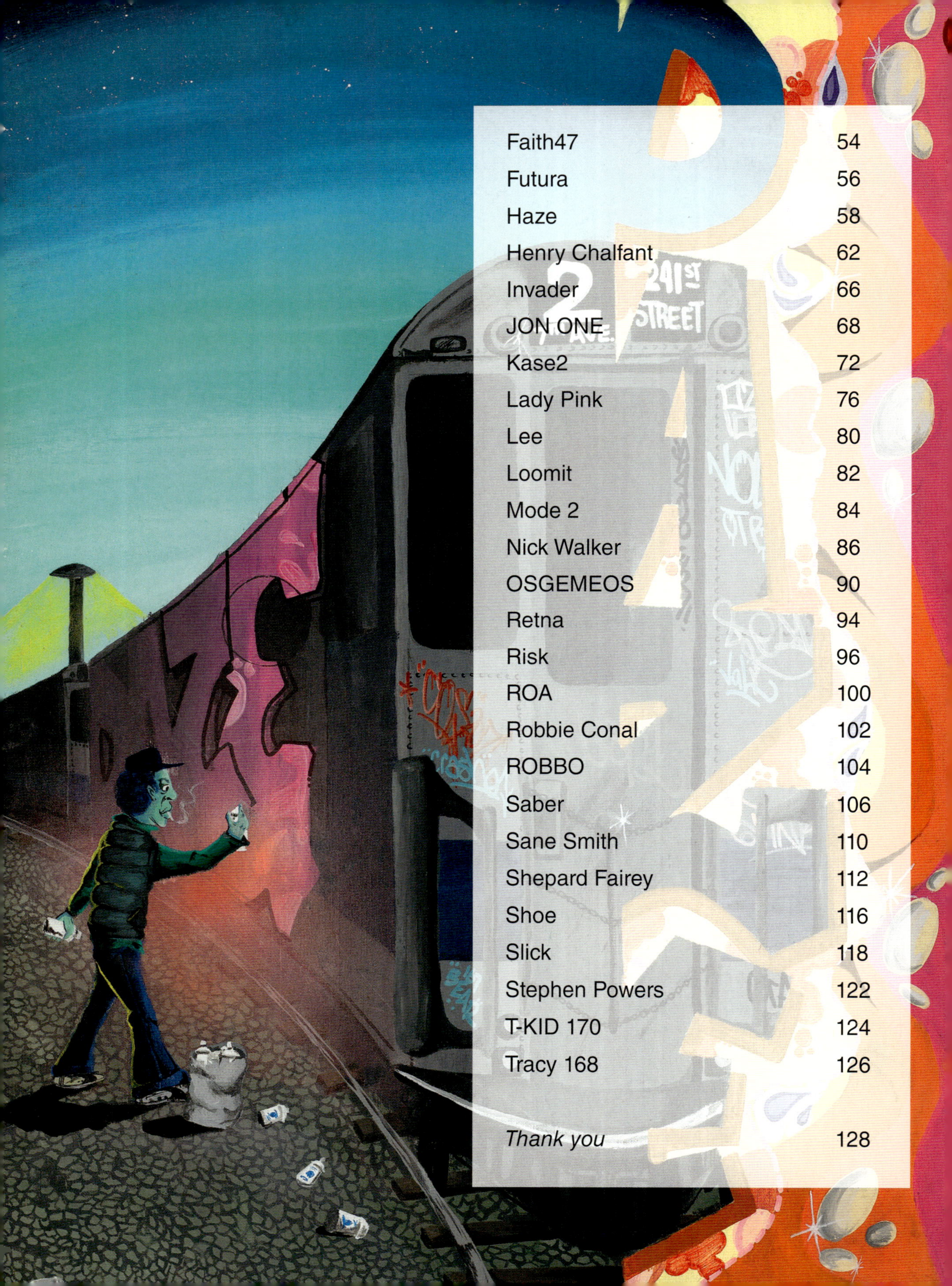

***Above*:** PART, Barcelona, Spain, 2009. Image courtesy of artist.

INTRODUCTION

Art can be found in urban spaces all across the world. Some of it comes from cooperation between local government, galleries and artists. It is public art as part of the orthodox art world, traditional and formal in structure, to be enjoyed in parks, High Streets and train stations everywhere. However, these urban spaces are also home to other types of art, many of them unsanctioned and even illegal, but also loved, and sometimes condemned, by the communities surrounding them. This book is about the artists who have pioneered, promoted and transformed this 'other' art world. By dedicating their talents and energy, they have achieved a level of fame and respect among their peers that makes them nothing less than 'legends'.

There are many styles of art to be found in city streets, and these have changed a great deal over the years. One type of art, however, has remained relevant and present since its adoption by the generation who grew up in the late 1960s: that art is 'writing', or as the general public knows it 'graffiti'. Its early appearance in Philadelphia, New York City and Los Angeles as a tagging movement was spearheaded by gangs and renegade teens such

as Cornbread and Julio 204. But it was the kids of New York City who turned it into an art movement, by taking simple names and adding flair, arrows and colours as embellishments. The practice spread so fast that by 1972 newspapers had criticized the activity as a virus among the city's youth. From 'tagging' (writing a stylized signature) to 'throw-ups' (designed for quick execution, with often simple, large bubble letters used to take up space) to more elaborate 'pieces' (larger, more time-intensive and colourful works), and lastly 'burners' ('pieces' that are so elaborate and impressive that they 'burn' the train or wall on which they are created), the proliferation of graffiti around the world is almost absolute. It is everywhere. And it has generated some of the key figures featured in this book, from early mavericks (like Tracy 168, BLADE, Futura, Haze and Lee), to the wave of giants who came to prominence in the 1980s (including Crash, Daze, T-KID 170 and Lady Pink), on to the great vandals of the 1990s (like Sane Smith

Left: Saber, skywriting protest, Los Angeles, USA, 2010. Photography by KET.
Below: Sento, Brooklyn, New York, USA, 2014. Image courtesy of artist.
Following pages: Kaws, Macy's promotion on New York City train, New York, USA, 2012. Photography by KET.

and Cost), and finally fast-forwarding to the writing movement's international stars (such as Mode 2, Shoe, Delta and Loomit). Their diversity of 'style', which demonstrates their own particular flair and originality, is beautiful to witness and a pleasure to share. All these artists came from humble art beginnings, many are self-taught, and all started out with a simple tag on a wall or train before becoming masters of their craft. They are the radicals of today's art world and, fortunately, many are finally getting the recognition they deserve.

Thanks to the rebellious nature of the writing and punk movements (whose do-it-yourself mentality embraced postering as promotion), urban art has never kept still for long. Among the many offshoots, one strain in particular – street art – has made real headway in terms of popularity and impact. Street art, which developed in the 1980s, is very different from the graffiti movement. Firstly, it is mostly character based or figurative (as opposed to letter based) and, secondly, it does not follow the same street codes that graffiti writers have so carefully established during their forty plus years in the business. For example, the code insists that writers do not paint over each other's work; doing so is regarded as a blatant act of intimidation or disrespect. Street artists do not interact with graffiti writers in that way and have at times covered graffiti works or incorporated them into new works, which has caused controversy and rancour between the two camps. But for all the quarrels and friction, street artists have managed to carve out a place for themselves on the streets, and have made a significant impact on the volume and diversity of styles that exist in urban spaces. Artists such as ROA, Invader and Blek le Rat have long been adding to the urban landscape with a wide range of techniques, including murals, mosaics, posters and stencils. Whereas in the graffiti movement spray paint and ink are the key tools, the street art movement has incorporated new mediums and methods that have allowed even the meekest art student to go outdoors and present art to the public.

Many street artists started out as writers (as is the case with Cost, Carolina Falkholt, Ben Eine, Nick Walker and Banksy), but others (like Robbie Conal and Shepard Fairey and thousands more) came to street art with no wider urban art background. However, due to their determination, and the popularity of their style of work, many have since become household names. Indeed, it is a testament to how far the wider urban art movement has come that graffiti writers and street artists alike have been able not only

to make an impact on the streets, but also develop careers as fine artists. Since the early gallery shows in New York City in the 1980s, in spaces like the Fun Gallery in the East Village and Fashion Moda in the Bronx, writers have exhibited alongside the established masters of the commercial art world. The success that these artists had in the 1980s – selling paintings to collectors worldwide – has laid down a blueprint for future generations of graffiti and street artists, and has demonstrated that there is a place for them and their style other than on the streets and trains.

This is not the definitive book on urban street art. The world of street art is so dynamic and fast-paced that the story is still being lived out. Inevitably, justice cannot be done to all those incredibly talented individuals who have informed and advocated the movement. The artists in this book are diverse, demonstrating the breadth and global impact of writing, style and street art, but there are many more who deserve recognition, with a special mention going to Cornbread, Part One, Sento, Revs, Seen, KAWS, Richard Hambleton, Phase 2, Iz the Wiz, Fuzz One, Quik, Dondi, Mad C, Dare, Bando, Wane, Martha Cooper, Reas, Binho, O'Clock, Miss Van, Elk, Egs, Stay High 149, Ghost, José Parlá, Riff 170, Erni Vales, Blu, the TATS Cru, Taps, Moses, the MUL crew, MOAS crew, Smash 137, Banos, Chintz, Mare139, NOC 167, DAIM and Rammellzee. I hope that the art in this book inspires you to discover more about the artists, and creates new fans for the most exciting art movement on the planet.

KET

TFP...
©2006...

TFP...
14...

Left: ATOME, Brooklyn, New York, USA, 2006. Photography by KET.
Bottom far left: ATOME, Sydney, Australia, 2014. Photography by artist.
Bottom left: ATOME, Bondi Beach, Sydney, Australia, 2012. Photography by artist.
Right: ATOME, Sydney, Australia, 2014. Photography by artist.

ATOME

As a teenager growing up in Sydney, ATOME experienced a broad cultural awakening in the early to mid 1980s, when he discovered the dynamic, youth-led world of hip-hop, breakdancing and rap music. But it was the thrill and adventure of the urban art scene that ensured graffiti writing would become the focus of his life.

Since then, ATOME has been credited as one of the first Australians to travel the globe extensively to write graffiti. In 1991 he set off on the first of his travels, excited by what had spilled out from the US and was now bubbling in Europe. What followed was a decade of exploring and painting intricate wildstyle pieces – sometimes in places, such as India, where graffiti art was still unknown.

Not that he has turned his back on his homeland. During the 1990s, ATOME was involved in Australia's first streetwear clothing label, and his crew were pioneers in Australian music and hip-hop culture publications.

Currently based in Sydney, ATOME continues to paint regularly and recently started to explore the possibility of bringing his art to other mediums.

BANKSY

Banksy is by far the most famous street artist. He is also the most reclusive, having kept his identity shrouded in mystery over the course of his whole career.

He began his artistic career much like the other urban legends: by painting his name as a graffiti writer. In Bristol, in the UK, Banksy was an early adopter of stencil art, he also moved away from the 'style' writing of traditional New York City graffiti art in favour of the 'street art' that is centred around figurative imagery. Along with artists such as Nick Walker and Blek le Rat, he popularized street art and became a leading figure in promoting the art form as an agent for creating social awareness. Banksy's style is unique, filled

LEGENDARY STATUS

In 2003 Banksy smuggled into Tate Britain an embellished oil painting, *Crimewatch UK Has Ruined the Countryside for All of Us*, a pastoral scene altered to include an incident scene sealed off with police tape.

with humour and a razor-sharp wit that targets a variety of issues and which at times seeks to represent the voice of the common man.

His studio practice informs his street art, and an impressive commitment to travel and spreading powerful messages has bolstered his reputation on a global scale. From Hurricane Katrina-scarred New Orleans to war-torn Gaza, Banksy's work appears where honest commentary is lacking, and because of his mainstream success his paintings cause such a stir that for a brief moment he is able to shift the conversation back to real ground-up problems.

Previous pages: Banksy, *Ghetto 4 Life*, Bronx, New York, USA, 2013. Photography by Ray Mock.
Above: Banksy, site-specific installation for Backjumps: the live issue, Kunstraum, Kreuzberg/Bethanien, Berlin, Germany, 2003. Image courtesy of Backjumps Archive.
Right: Banksy, *Toxic Mary*, screen print on paper, 69.9 x 50.2 c.m., 2004. Private collection.

Left**:** Ben Eine in action, Bronx, New York, USA, 2011. Photography by KET.
Above**:** Ben Eine, *Vandals*, Miami, Florida, USA, 2012. Photography by KET.

LEGENDARY STATUS

In July 2010, during a state visit to Washington, the British Prime Minister, David Cameron, presented Barack Obama with a painting by Eine, *Twenty First Century City*, as an official gift.

BEN EINE

Ben Eine (Ben Flynn, born in 1970) is best known for his giant typography and statement-based murals, as well as alphabet paintings on shop shutters. Prior to becoming involved in commercial and fine art, Eine was a highly credible graffiti writer in the London urban scene, putting in over twenty years of work on the streets and city trains. His stylized bubble letters stood out from the usual tags seen on the streets, and can still be found in some areas of east London.

Eine first gained recognition via his close relationship with Bristol-based street artist Banksy. While Banksy was able to bring Eine into the commercial art world, in exchange, Eine opened doors to the underground scene. In 2010, he painted the complete alphabet on Middlesex Street in east London, which was rechristened Alphabet Street by the residents, and his colourful and bright letters and wry statements have transformed streets around the world in cities such as Los Angeles, San Francisco, Mexico City, Tokyo, London and Stockholm, as well as New York City.

LEGENDARY STATUS

Over the course of his career, BLADE has painted over 5000 graffiti pieces on subway trains in New York City.

BLADE

BLADE (Steven Ogburn, born in 1957) is a Bronx graffiti legend who began his career in 1972, during the early days of New York City's graffiti movement, by painting the local area's buses and trains. He is a founding member of the prolific TC5 (The Crazy Five) crew and, along with his partner Comet, he has painted thousands of subway cars along the 2 and 5 train lines (the most prestigious of all of New York City's train lines for showcasing art). BLADE's trains were some of the most creative and beautiful to be seen on the city's tracks, and included a wide range of cartoon characters, scenes and lettering. By 1980 he was considered the undisputed king of graffiti.

In 1984, BLADE gave up painting trains and began to paint exclusively on canvas for galleries in Europe. His new paintings reflected the same energy as his train art, and further demonstrated his ability to combine psychedelic themes with an audacious flair for lettering. BLADE's fine art has taken him around the world with permanent collections housed in the Groninger Museum in the Netherlands, the Experience Music Project Museum in Seattle, and the Brooklyn Museum and the Museum of the City of New York. In 2011, he also participated in the largest museum event dedicated to graffiti, 'Art in the Streets', at the MOCA (Museum of Contemporary Art) in Los Angeles.

Left: BLADE, *Gangster*, whole car subway train, Bronx, New York, USA, *c*. 1980. Photography by artist.
Above: BLADE, *Happiness Is*, spray paint on canvas, 185 x 215 c.m., 1983. Speerstra Collection.
Right: BLADE, *Pisstolini*, whole car subway train, Bronx, New York, USA, *c*. 1978. Photography by artist.

BLEK LE RAT

Blek le Rat (Xavier Prou, born in 1951) was one of the first graffiti artists in Paris, and the originator of stencil graffiti art. He took his graffiti name from a comic book character called Blek le Roc, while the 'Rat' part acts as an anagram of 'art'.

Blek's early art was truly pioneering; he broke away from the popular New York graffiti style to develop work that he felt better suited the atmosphere and architecture of Parisian streets. He began working in 1981, stencilling images of rats onto the street walls of Paris. To Blek, the rat was 'the only free animal in the city', and was particularly appropriate as an urban emblem as it 'spreads the plague everywhere, just like street art'.

Blek is perhaps most famous for being credited as the inventor of the life-sized stencil, as well as being the first artist to use stencilling to create pictorial art. Prior to this, stencils had largely only been used to create lettering. In this he would pave the way for others such as Banksy, Nick Walker, ADW and Logan Hicks, making stencilling a ubiquitous branch of urban art.

In 1991 Blek was arrested by the French police for stencilling a replica of Caravaggio's 'Madonna and Child'. During the episode Blek's real identity was uncovered and made public. Since then, he has mainly worked with

BLEK LE RAT

pre-stencilled posters, extolling the benefits of the speedier application of the medium to walls, as well as the advantage of a reduced punishment should he be caught in the act.

Recently, Blek's work has become more political in focus, the environment and social issues being major sources of inspiration. In particular, Blek has sought to bring attention to the homeless, a matter he regards to be a crisis on a global scale. In 2005, he began creating a series of images which depict the homeless standing, sitting or lying on pavements. That same year he also designed posters of kidnapped French journalist Florence Aubenas, helping to raise public awareness and pressure politicians and journalists to work harder for her release.

***Previous pages*:** Blek le Rat, Brooklyn, New York, USA, 2014. Photography by KET.
***Left*:** Blek le Rat, *Old Man*, Paris, France, 1983. Image courtesy of artist.
***Right top*:** Blek le Rat, *Soldier*, Berlin Wall, Berlin, Germany, 2003. Image courtesy of artist.
***Right bottom*:** Blek le Rat, Brooklyn, New York, USA, 2014. Photography by KET.

日本地区への迂回路
DETOUR TO THE
JAPANESE SECTOR

CAROLINA FALKHOLT

Carolina Falkholt (born in 1977) is an acclaimed Swedish artist. She started her graffiti career in New York City in the 1990s under her alias Blue as a member of The Fantastic Partners and Hardcore Chicks, working together with painters such as Sento, Kase2, Daze and Lady Pink.

Since the late 1990s, Falkholt has developed her graffiti style in combination with performance and music, bringing them together in social spaces and regularly inviting other artists, musicians, organizations and the public into collaborations. Apart from spray painting and drawing, she also makes sculptures, performs, writes lyrics and music, and creates videos. Falkholt explores not only her own aesthetic expression, but also the social possibilities of graffiti in the gap between graffiti as subculture and graffiti as contemporary art.

LEGENDARY STATUS

Falkholt became famous worldwide after her abstract mural *Snippmålning*, which depicted vaginas, went on display on the wall of the Tessin High School in Nyköping, just outside Stockholm.

***Above*:** Carolina Falkholt, *Övermålning* (*Overpainted*), Nyköping, Sweden, 2014. Photography by Patrik Ljungman.

She tends to work in large-scale form through improvisation, dealing with topics like contemporary social issues and local history. Her firm standpoints about issues such as feminism and artistic freedom, and the fact that her work takes up substantial public spaces, has often put her at the heart of heated debates.

Falkholt's gallery work is housed all over Sweden, in the collections of the Gothenburg Museum of Art, Skövde Art Museum and the Halland Museum of Cultural History. Her public work appears in many Swedish cities, including Uppsala, Borås, Nyköping, Simrishamn, Luleå, Mariestad, Avesta, Visby and Halmstad. Recently, she has made monumental paintings in Durrës in Albania, Rovaniemi in Finland, Severomorsk in Russia, Cairo in Egypt and Amman in Jordan.

TFP..
2011..

COPE2

Cope2 (Fernando Carol Jr, born in 1968) is a widely celebrated legend who has contributed over thirty years to the graffiti and street art scene. One of New York City's most prolific graffiti artists, he began tagging his name in the South Bronx in 1978 at the age of just ten. He developed his style in the subways alongside the internationally renowned KD crew and was inspired by the great writers of the Bronx, such as Mitch77, Kel1st, T-KID 170 and Ban2. During his subway heyday he painted insides, pieces and throw-ups, and had epic graffiti wars with the pioneering RIS and MPC crews.

When the New York City graffiti movement moved away from the trains and into the streets in the late 1980s, Cope2 began organizing large-scale graffiti murals, bringing together artists from all over the world to collaborate on monumental art works in the Bronx. By the 1990s he had achieved international recognition for his distinctive style and prodigious output.

In recent years Cope2 has moved into the studio in order to create timeless pieces for collectors, as well as taking commissions from a broad range of companies including *Time* magazine, Converse and Adidas. His work has even crossed into the virtual realm with appearances in video games such as Mark Ecko's 'Getting up: Contents Under Pressure' and Rockstar Games' 'Grand Theft Auto IV'. Today, you can catch Cope2 painting in the studio, bringing his raw energy into abstract expressionist style masterpieces, intertwined with his trademark bubble letters and tags.

Previous pages left: Cope2, classic throw-ups, New Design High School, New York, USA, 2011. Photography by KET.

Previous pages right: Cope2, Bagnolet, Paris, France, 2005. Photography by KET.

Above: Cope2, Brooklyn, New York, USA, 2010. Photography by KET.

Below: Cope2, panel piece, Bronx, New York, USA, *c*. 1982. Image courtesy of artist.

***Above*:** Cope2, Bronx, New York, USA, 2005. Image courtesy of artist.
***Below*:** Cope2, Bronx, New York, USA, 2011. Photography by KET.

COST WAS HERE
COST WAS HERE
COST WAS HERE
COST
REVS
COST
IS SO
ORCHARD*
The Pope of Trash
COST
ENX
Talk As Dirty As You Want & I will Do The Same
COST
COST

COST

Adam Cost began his career in the early 1980s in New York City's subways, but moved above ground in the 1990s, when he would ultimately transform the art world's perceptions and standards. Cost, along with his cohort Revs, introduced different mediums (such as postering) to the post-train graffiti culture and led the growth of the street art scene to the point where it has become an international phenomenon. The result? A redefinition of what is now currently known as the street art movement.

His poster campaigns, huge sprawling rollers (using house paint and rollers), street paintings in doorways, canvas installations, stencils, paintings and stickers have altered the entire New York City landscape and inspired a new generation of artists to follow suit. There was a time when you couldn't cross a New York City intersection without seeing a piece of his cryptic work attached to the back of a traffic light.

Now in his forties, he remains active in his street rituals, while contributing to the ever-changing New York City landscape through guerilla art tactics. As more space is occupied and many artists emulate his style, Cost continues to stand out as one of the best. Through sheer effort, ability and know-how, his work raises the bar time and time again.

Previous pages left: Cost and Enx, door smashes with posters, Brooklyn, New York, USA, 2013. Photography by Luna Park.
Previous pages right: Cost and Revs, Soho, New York, USA, 2000. Photography by KET.
Above: Cost, Brooklyn, New York, USA, 2012. Photography by Luna Park.
Right: Cost, New York, USA, 2012. Photography by Luna Park.
Opposite page: Cost, flypaper box, New York, USA, 2009. Photography by Ray Mock.

AVALON CHEMISTS
212.260.3131
WE DELIVER
AVALON CHEMISTS
YOUR PRESCRIPTION
COST
ADAM
ORCHARD
COST FUCKED MADONNA
PAINT
DEATH
COST
WAS FIRST
COST FUCKED REVS
GADFLY
COST

LEGENDARY STATUS

Crash's trains first appeared in print on the cover of the graffiti bible *Subway Art*, catapulting him to international fame and making his art the object of every young urban artist's ambition.

Above: Daze and Crash, The L.I.S.A. Project, New York, USA, 2014. Image courtesy of artist.
Below: Crash, *Crash Boom*, spray paint on canvas, 130 x 240 c.m., 1983. Speerstra Collection.

CRASH

Crash (John Matos, born in 1961) was raised in the Bronx, New York City. At the age of thirteen, he started to follow the older teens from his neighbourhood to the train yards where he began bombing. Taking the name Crash after he accidentally crashed his school's computer, his tag soon began appearing on trains circulating throughout New York City. At the height of his graffiti career he painted alongside some of the best artists of his generation, including Kase2, Daze and Kel1st. As a writer who played with letterforms, Crash's graffiti styles ranged from complex burners ('masterpieces') to plain letters and thematic pieces.

By 1980, he was transitioning from painting in train yards to exhibiting in art galleries. That year he curated the groundbreaking exhibition 'Graffiti Art Success for America' at Fashion Moda in the Bronx, pioneering the graffiti movement's relationship with the gallery world. With that show, Crash's career took off and he gained instant popularity throughout Europe and the United States, and eventually Asia. Since then, Crash's work has been part of numerous museum and gallery shows around the world, and it is included in many permanent museum collections. Due to his visually iconic imagery, he has partnered with all types of companies on a variety of projects, including Absolut Vodka, Fender Guitars, Sobella Handbags and Levi's.

In the past decade he has returned to painting traditional graffiti and murals in New York City, bringing his style back into the streets for a new generation to admire.

***Above, top*:** Crash, panel piece on subway train, Bronx, New York, USA, 1980. Photography by Phade.

***Above*:** Crash, *Smoking*, spray paint on canvas, 130 x 245 c.m., 1981. Speerstra Collection.

***Right*:** Crash, *Remains of the Day*, spray paint on canvas, 208 x 168 c.m., 2012. Private collection.

DAZE

Chris 'Daze' Ellis (born in Brooklyn in 1962), began his prolific career painting the New York City subways in the mid 1970s while attending the city's High School of Art and Design. During his time as a subway artist he painted alongside the best artists of his generation, including Mitch, Crash, Dez and Skeme.

Turning his focus from trains to canvas in the early 1980s, his first group show, 'Beyond Words', was held at the Mudd Club in New York City in 1981, where he exhibited alongside artists such as Jean-Michel Basquiat and Keith Haring. Daze sold his first work – an impromptu collaboration with Basquiat – from that show. His first solo show was held a year later, in 1982, at Fashion Moda. Since then he has had many solo shows all over the world.

Despite this move into the commercial art scene Daze's commitment to public art remains fresh. Daze's many accomplishments

PALACE
DAZE
4 5 6 Exit

include completing a mural for the Star Ferry terminal in Hong Kong, lecturing at Hofstra University in Long Island and the Bronx Museum in New York City, designing an entire train station in Hanover, Germany (together with Lee and Crash), conducting youth workshops during the Hutuz Rap Festival in Rio de Janeiro, and painting a mural for the VivoCity shopping mall in Singapore.

Daze's paintings have been bought by the likes of Madonna and Eric Clapton, and his work can be found in the permanent collections of the Museum of Modern Art in New York City, the Brooklyn Museum, the Museum of the City of New York, the Groninger Museum in the Netherlands and Museum Ludwig in Germany.

Today, Daze continues to live and work in New York City, contributing his bold and funky lettering style and soulful characters to the city landscape. As a master illustrator, he embellishes his graffiti pieces with a rich and diverse cast of characters, which makes his art accessible to both the sophisticated graffiti follower and the uninitiated. His pieces remain among the best in New York City.

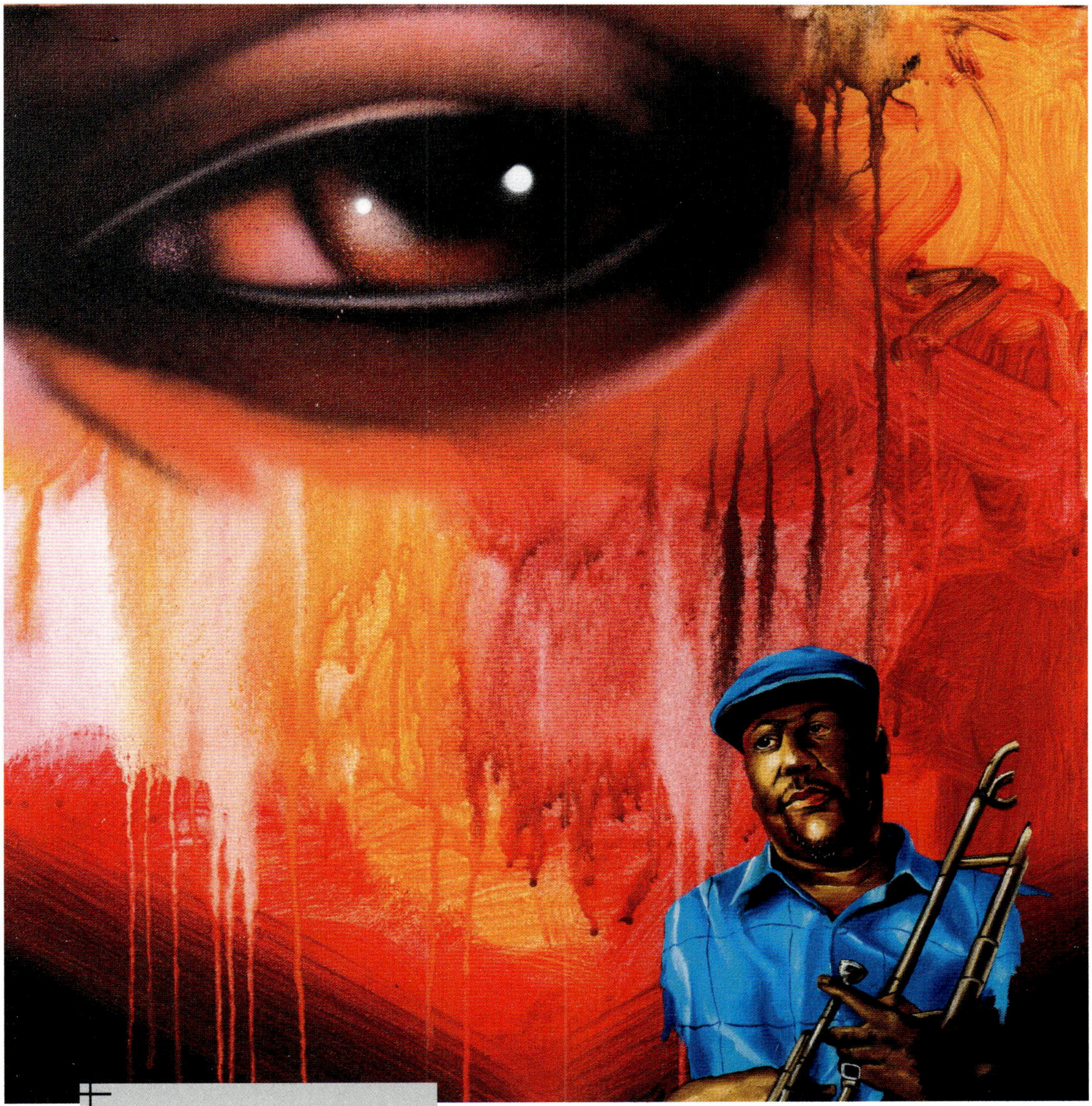

LEGENDARY STATUS

Daze appeared in the groundbreaking documentary *Style Wars* in 1983 and in the graffiti bible *Subway Art*, which made his style one of the most copied in the graffiti world.

Previous pages left: Daze, Brooklyn, New York, USA, 2009. Photography by KET.

Previous pages right: Daze, *Velocity*, spray paint, acrylic, pumice and oil on canvas, 183 x 183 c.m., 2014. Image courtesy of artist.

Left: Daze, *Hotel Amazon*, acrylic on canvas, 168 x 224 c.m., 1988. Museum of the City of New York / Martin Wong Collection.

Above: Daze, *From Across the Room*, oil, acrylic and spray paint on canvas, 61 x 261 c.m., 2014. Image courtesy of artist.

DELTA

Delta (Boris Tellegen, born in 1968) is an artist who currently lives and works in his native city of Amsterdam. He became a graffiti artist in the 1980s, and was immediately fixated on the idea of breaking free of the flat surface he was painting on by using letter designs in a three-dimensional way. His unique style – traditional graffiti letters blended with his own three-dimensional twist and sense of humour – together with his strong output gained him recognition and respect among his peers.

Since the 1980s his focus has been drawn to walls, with the odd train here and there, but his approach has been very different to that of other artists who were working at the same time. Early on in his career he started experimenting with different mediums and surfaces, all in the pursuit of transcending the two-dimensionality of concrete walls. He learned how to bend mediums to give them depth, and this style has characterized his career over the last thirty years.

While studying Industrial Design

Engineering at TU Delft, from where he graduated in 1994, he had a breakthrough. Using the skills he learned in architecture and design, he could finally escape the plane with sculpturally driven works that used space to draw viewers into his creations. In particular, Delta began looking at architectural plans and city layouts, which led to the creation of what he termed his 'isometric industrial landscapes'. Each of these sculptures combines thick layers of building materials that start out as scattered salvaged junk and combine to form clean, crisp shapes. From the front the work appears to be a flat plane of geometric shapes; however, upon closer inspection from the side, the viewer can see that Delta has carefully built up layer upon layer of materials with varying depths and textures.

Having worked in collage, sculpture, drawings, paintings, videos and installations, Delta today continues to create mixed-media sculptures via private commissions in his native Netherlands and exhibits his art globally.

Below left: Delta, freight train piece, Amsterdam, Holland, 2014. Image courtesy of artist.
Below right: Delta, *charleroi2*, statue, Charleroi, Belgium, 2014. Image courtesy of artist.

Above: Delta, *Kunstraum*, installation in Kunstraum Basel, Basel, Switzerland, 2011. Private collection.
Below: Delta, *a1fotopetercox*, installation at De Fabriek, Eindhoven, Netherlands, 2011. Private collection.
Right: Delta, *Issues IV*, acrylic on 8 layers of birch wood, 120 x 90 x 9 c.m., 2015. Private collection.

Far left: Doze Green, *Rise Above Vegas* mural, Las Vegas, Nevada, USA, 2014. Image courtesy of artist.
Left: Doze Green, *Saafia and the Arcons*, mixed mediums on canvas, 153 x 178 c.m., 2014. Image courtesy of artist.

LEGENDARY STATUS

Doze, as a member of the Rock Steady Crew, released *Ready for Battle*, a rap and electro album in 1984.

DOZE GREEN

In 1976, Doze Green (Jeffrey Green, born in 1964) began painting New York City subway cars and became one of the original b-boy (break dancer) members of the Rock Steady Crew, a group that would become famous for their dance style. His train painting exploits took place alongside the TC5 and IBM crews, who at the time dominated the trains in Manhattan. Doze is recognized for creating the prototypical b-boy character image, based on the b-boy Ken Swift, which is still a staple of graffiti style illustration. After his subway painting career ended in the early 1980s, he transitioned to studio work and mural commissions.

In his role as a fine artist Green's paintings blend the b-boy and graffiti world with the metaphysical and esoteric.

Above: Doze Green, *Out of Knowwhere the Power*, mixed mediums on canvas, 76 x 76 c.m., 2014. Private collection.

Right: Doze Green, *MARDUK*, mixed mediums on canvas, 101 x 76 c.m., 2013. Private collection.

His paintings have the familiar flow of a dance, of action, but his technique is so refined that it's easy to mistake for chaos. He's one part Cubist, one part abstract artist, b-boy and elder graffiti statesman.

Recent projects include a large-scale mural painted during São Paulo Fashion Week in Brazil, a public mural titled *Crossroads of Humanity* located at CityCenter in Las Vegas, Nevada, and a whole train project that he worked on in collaboration with OSGEMEOS, again in Brazil.

Above: Drax (with ROBBO), whole train, London, UK, 1989. Image courtesy of artist.
Right: Drax, Mumbai, India, 2008. Image courtesy of artist.

DRAX

Drax first became interested in graffiti writing when he watched the 1979 gangland film *The Warriors*, and by 1984, after watching the urban art documentary *Style Wars*, he was hooked. By the following year Drax had chosen his tag and had begun writing on the streets of London. During the late 1980s and early 1990s he was considered one of the most prevalent writers on the city's streets, and had also painted a few trains. A handful of these, such as the whole train he painted with ROBBO in 1989, are now among the most famous painted trains in London's graffiti history. Consequently, he attracted the attention of the British Transport Police and was prosecuted for vandalism in 1991. Narrowly avoiding a prison sentence, from that point onwards he did

most of his painting abroad, most famously in 1992, when he and ROBBO painted together on the New York City subway.

By the end of the 1990s Drax was bored with his London writing career, so he embraced a concept he calls 'Graff tourism' and set about travelling to the furthest reaches of the planet in order to sign his name in the most exotic and unreachable locations. He has to date painted some form of graffiti (legal and illegal) in six continents and approximately seventy-five countries. In a career spanning over thirty years, he has never had the urge to give up, and despite the fact that he will be fifty years old this year, he still embraces the slogan, 'Old enough to know better, but still young enough to fucking love it!'

Above: Drax, Phnom Penh, Cambodia, 2009. Image courtesy of artist.
Right: Drax, Kampala, Uganda, 2010. Image courtesy of artist.
Top far right: Drax, *Electro Magnetic Intercourse (Acid Rave Train)*, London, UK, 1989. Image courtesy of artist.
Bottom far right: Drax, *Infected by the Germs of Life*, London, UK, 1991. Image courtesy of artist.

NO SMOKING
ELECTRO

FAITH47

Faith47 is an internationally acclaimed street- and studio-based artist currently living in Cape Town, South Africa.

Following an active street art career spanning more than fifteen years, her work can now be found in major cities around the world. Using a wide range of mediums, including graphite, spray paint, oil paint, ink, photography and collage, her approach is explorative and bends to the surface on which she is working – from found and rescued objects, to history-blemished city walls and studio-prepared canvas and wood.

Through her work, Faith47 attempts to advance the expression of personal truth offering both an internal and spiritual release that speaks to the complexities of the human condition.

Faith47's first solo exhibition, 'Fragments of a Burnt History', was held at the David Krut Gallery in Johannesburg in 2012. Using an immersive environment, it explored the transformation of Johannesburg into a more representative African city, exposing the harsh realities of day-to-day life and capturing the remnants of South Africa's complex history in a personal and symbolic manner.

Her 2014 solo exhibition in London, 'Aqua Regalia', further extended the possibilities of immersive spaces, enveloping the viewer into a sacred room filled with collected objects from everyday life that – together with figurative paintings – explored the notion of the mundane and unwanted as sacred.

Above: Faith47, *Landfill Meditation*, Athlone, Cape Town, South Africa, 2015. Image courtesy of artist.
Right: Faith47, *Capax Infiniti*, Portland, Oregon, USA, 2014. Image courtesy of artist.

POTHOLE
HOTLINE
503-823-BUMP
(823-2867)
City of Portland

Left**:** Futura, *Interkosmos*, spray paint on canvas, 274 x 213 c.m., 1984. Collection of C. C. McGurr.
Above**:** Futura, tag, neon lighting, 2012. Private collection.
Right**:** Futura, *Benghazi*, spray paint and latex on canvas, 91 x 91 c.m., 2011. Private collection.

FUTURA

Futura (formerly known as Futura 2000, born Leonard McGurr in 1955) started out as a graffiti writer at the age of fifteen, exercising his craft on New York City's walls and subways. As graffiti art started to make its presence known, a good stylized signature (tag) was a major ambition for artists, and Futura had one of the best.

In the late 1970s, after a brief hiatus to join the Navy, he returned to New York and reinvented himself, pioneering abstract art while the majority of other graffiti artists concentrated on lettering. His 'Break' trains represented a completely new direction away from traditional graffiti, and they set the stage for his career as a fine artist.

His first group show took place in 1981 at the SA Alternative Space, in New York City. Soon after, he was on the Clash's 1981 European tour painting live backdrops on stage, and in 1982 he exhibited at the Fun Gallery, along with Keith Haring, Jean-Michel Basquiat, Richard Hambleton and Kenny Scharf. This led to further exhibitions worldwide.

In the 1990s Futura reinvented himself yet again as a clothing designer, and launched a succession of successful streetwear brands. Recon and Project Dragon were particularly well received and he went on to collaborate with brands such as A Bathing Ape, Mo' Wax, and Nike. By the turn of the century he had developed a global cult following among sneaker fans.

LEGENDARY STATUS

Haze's first tag, SE3, dominated the New York City subways in the early 1980s when he was a member of the Rolling Thunder Writers crew. His throw-up is widely considered one of the best.

Left: Haze, mural, Hong Kong, China, 2007. Image courtesy of artist.
Right: Haze as SE3, top to bottom throw-up, New York Subway, New York, USA, 1982. Image courtesy of artist.

HAZE

Born in 1961, native New Yorker Eric Haze has been making his impact felt in the worlds of art, design and product for over three decades. As an original member of the Soul Artists and Zoo York skate crew, Haze was one of the first generation of legitimate graffiti artists to emerge into the art world in the early 1980s. Featured in Richard Goldstein's seminal *Village Voice* article 'Graffiti Above Ground' (which for the first time revealed the identity of the graffiti writers who were crossing over into the art world), Haze went on to exhibit artwork alongside the likes of Keith Haring, Jean-Michel Basquiat and Andy Warhol in 'New York, New Wave' at the exhibition space PS1. He has also shown his work in transformational galleries of the era, such as the Fun Gallery.

With a continued passion for lettering and the written word, Haze switched gears in the mid 1980s, studying design at the School of Visual Arts in New York City, and preparing himself to take on a new focus in the world of graphic design and art direction.

Upon setting up his first design studio in 1985, Haze quickly became recognized as one of the few graphic artists to emerge from the original hip-hop movement. He went on to uniquely define the image and visual style of hip-hop's golden age by creating logos, album covers and identities for artists like Public Enemy, the Beastie Boys, LL Cool J, EPMD, Young MC and Tone-Lōc. He also created artwork for influential record labels like Delicious Vinyl, Cold Chillin' and Def Jam. Having produced designs for fashion icons like Vision Street Wear and Swatch, in 1992 the emerging school of US independent clothing companies also began calling, and Haze moved shop to Los Angeles, where he founded his own clothing brand, Haze.

The turn of the century saw Haze once again leading the design pack and collaborating with industry leaders such as Nike, G-Shock and Honda, ushering in the era of artist-driven limited editions for products as diverse as watches, cars, jewellery, skateboards, furniture and footwear. The new millennium also saw an inspired return by Haze to his fine art roots, including four solo exhibitions in Hong Kong, New York and Los Angeles, as well as an installation of his iconic design work in MOCA's (Museum of Contemporary Art) 2011 'Art in the Streets' exhibition.

At present, Haze continues to direct his brand and design studio out of his company's Williamsburg, Brooklyn headquarters.

Left: Haze x Nike, Dunk High and Low, 2003. Image courtesy of artist.

Above: Haze, tag on inside of a New York City subway car, New York, USA, 1982. Image courtesy of artist.

Below: Haze, Standard Hotel mural, Los Angeles, California, USA, 2011. Image courtesy of artist.

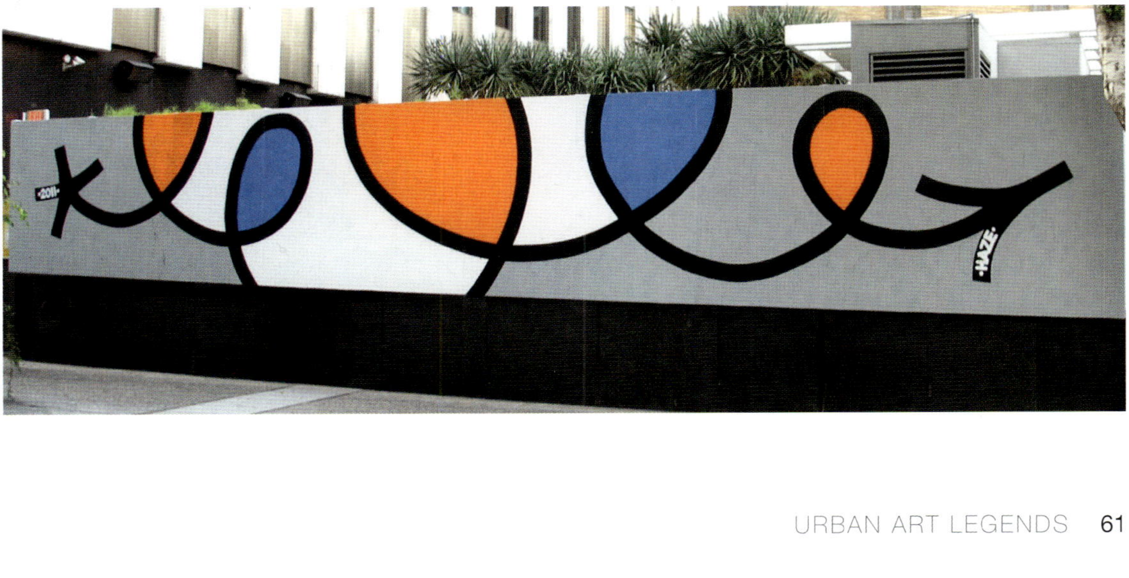

***Above*:** Noc167, *Style Wars* whole car subway train, New York, USA, 1981. Photography by Henry Chalfant.
***Below*:** Kel 139, *Dealt Kel 139 Henry* subway train, New York, USA, 1980. Photography by Henry Chalfant.

***Following pages left*:** Henry Chalfant, *Rock Steady Crew*, New York, USA, 1981. Photography by Henry Chalfant.
***Following pages right*:** Henry Chalfant, *Min One in the New Lots train yard*, Brooklyn, New York, USA, 1980. Photography by Henry Chalfant.

HENRY CHALFANT

Henry Chalfant (born in 1940 in Pennsylvania) has taken hundreds of photographs documenting a huge variety of original urban art works that have long since vanished. Starting out as a sculptor in New York City in the 1970s, he turned to photography and film in order to create an in-depth study of hip-hop culture and graffiti art. Regarded as one of the foremost authorities on New York City subway art and other aspects of urban youth culture, his photos are in the permanent collection of the Museum of Modern Art in New York City and the Museum of the City of New York. He has co-authored the definitive account of New York City's graffiti art, *Subway Art* (1984), and a sequel on the art form's worldwide diffusion, *Spray Can Art* (1987). Film has also played a key part in his career. Among others, Chalfant co-produced the PBS documentary *Style Wars* (1983), the ultimate documentary about graffiti and hip-hop culture, and directed *Flyin' Cut Sleeves* (1993), a documentary on South Bronx gangs. *Subway Art* and *Style Wars* became for many eager youths their first introduction to the graffiti world and served as a catalyst for the adoption of graffiti art worldwide, making him and his co-author, Martha Cooper, cult icons.

Above left**:** Invader, High Line, New York, USA, 2013. Photography by Luna Park.
Above right**:** Invader, Miami, Florida, USA, 2013. Photography by KET.
Right**:** Invader, *Snow White*, New York, USA, 2013. Photography by Luna Park.
Far right**:** Invader, Brooklyn, New York, USA, 2010. Photography by KET.

LEGENDARY STATUS

In Invader's latest and greatest installation, his work has been sent to space. Thanks to the European Space Agency's cooperation, *Space2* is now permanently installed aboard the International Space Station.

INVADER

Invader (also called Space Invader) is a French artist born in 1969 who is known for affixing mosaic tile images of characters from the 1970s video game 'Space Invaders' to city walls around the world. Once a work is installed Invader records it as an 'invasion', and then creates accompanying maps and reference books to indicate the location of each piece. Invader began these urban installations in Paris in 1998, and continued to 'invade' thirty-one other cities in France, followed by an additional thirty-two cities across the planet.

The mosaics are made using weather-resistant tiles, which represent the pixels used for graphics in early video and computer games. One of the most conspicuous locations to feature his works is the landmark Hollywood Sign in Los Angeles, California; the first mosaic work was mounted on the 'D' letter on 31 December 1999. Since 2000, Invader's works have featured in galleries around the world garnering fans and great reviews alike.

JON ONE

JON ONE (John Andrew Perello, born in 1963) was raised in Harlem, New York City, where his train paintings are widely considered some of the best ever created, following in the tradition of the great train masters Lee and BLADE. Thanks to the recognition he gained from his early work on the trains, in 1984 JON ONE created – with the support of several other committed graffiti artists – the renowned international crew 156 All Starz. It was also as a subway artist that he began to experiment and break away from the traditional graffiti style that was popular at the time, creating complex letterforms that were abstract and illegible, early innovations that he would carry throughout his career.

During his early years, he met his French counterpart, Bando, who quickly invited him to join him in Paris. JON ONE fell in love with Paris and its hip-hop

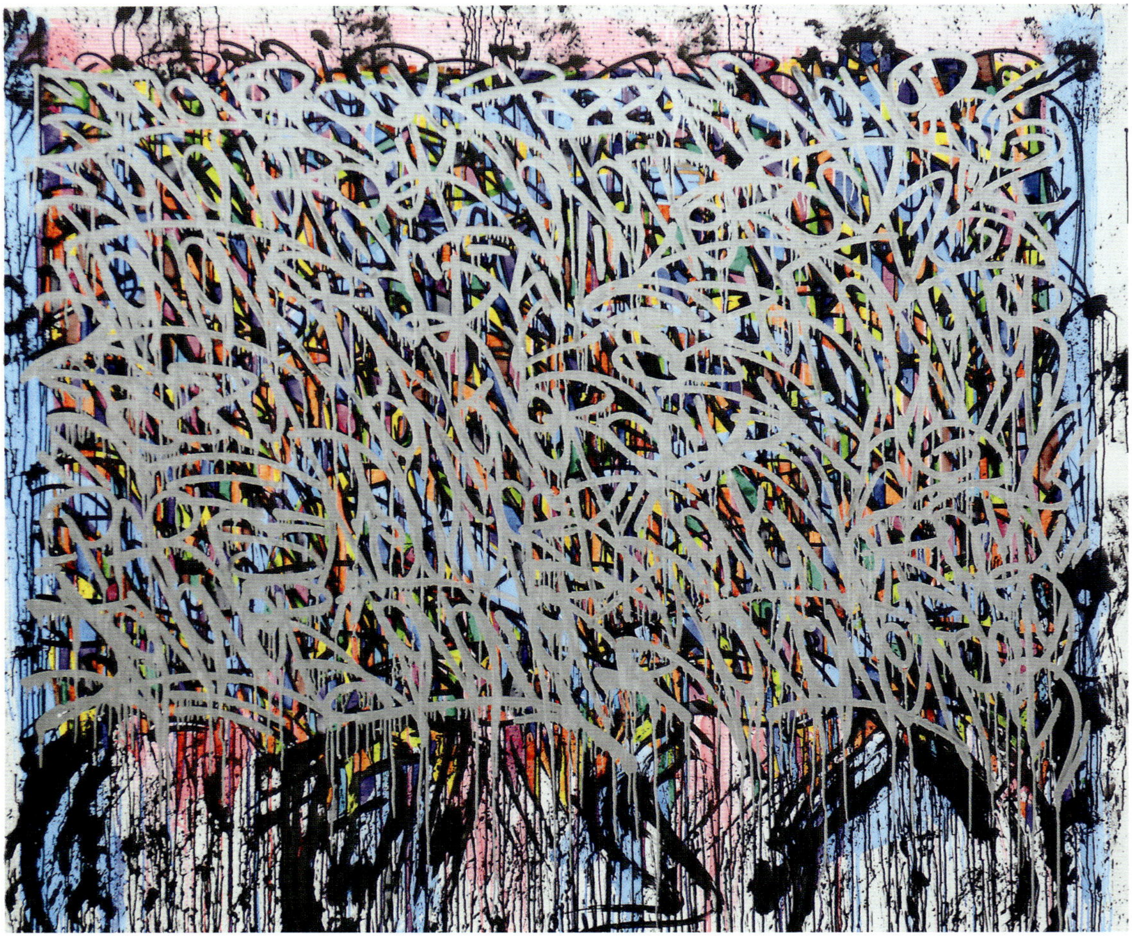

***Left*:** JON ONE, *A Dream: Then I Woke Up*, ink and acrylic on canvas, 170 x 210 c.m., 2008. Image courtesy of artist.

***Above*:** JON ONE, *Le Départ*, spray paint and acrylic on canvas, 600 x 300 c.m., 1994. Speerstra Collection.

***Below*:** JON ONE, New York City subway piece, New York, USA, 1986. Photography by KET.

LEGENDARY STATUS

In 2015 JON ONE received France's premier award, the Legion of Honour, recognizing his contribution to art and culture in France.

culture, and started to produce paintings on canvas for the first time. His relocation to France introduced the possibility of becoming a full-time fine artist, and he embraced the opportunity wholeheartedly. His pieces have been exhibited internationally in places such as Tokyo, Monaco, New York City and Hong Kong. Whether in the street or in a museum, JON ONE has complete control over his aesthetic language that is one part traditional graffiti and the other abstract painting. His mash-ups of multiple styles were considered strange at the time, but today the world has finally caught up.

***Left*:** JON ONE, throw-up on store gate, Harlem, New York, USA, *c.* 2000. Photography by KET.
***Below*:** JON ONE, *Poetry of Colors*, spray paint and acrylic on canvas, 130 x 112 c.m., 1992. Speerstra Collection.

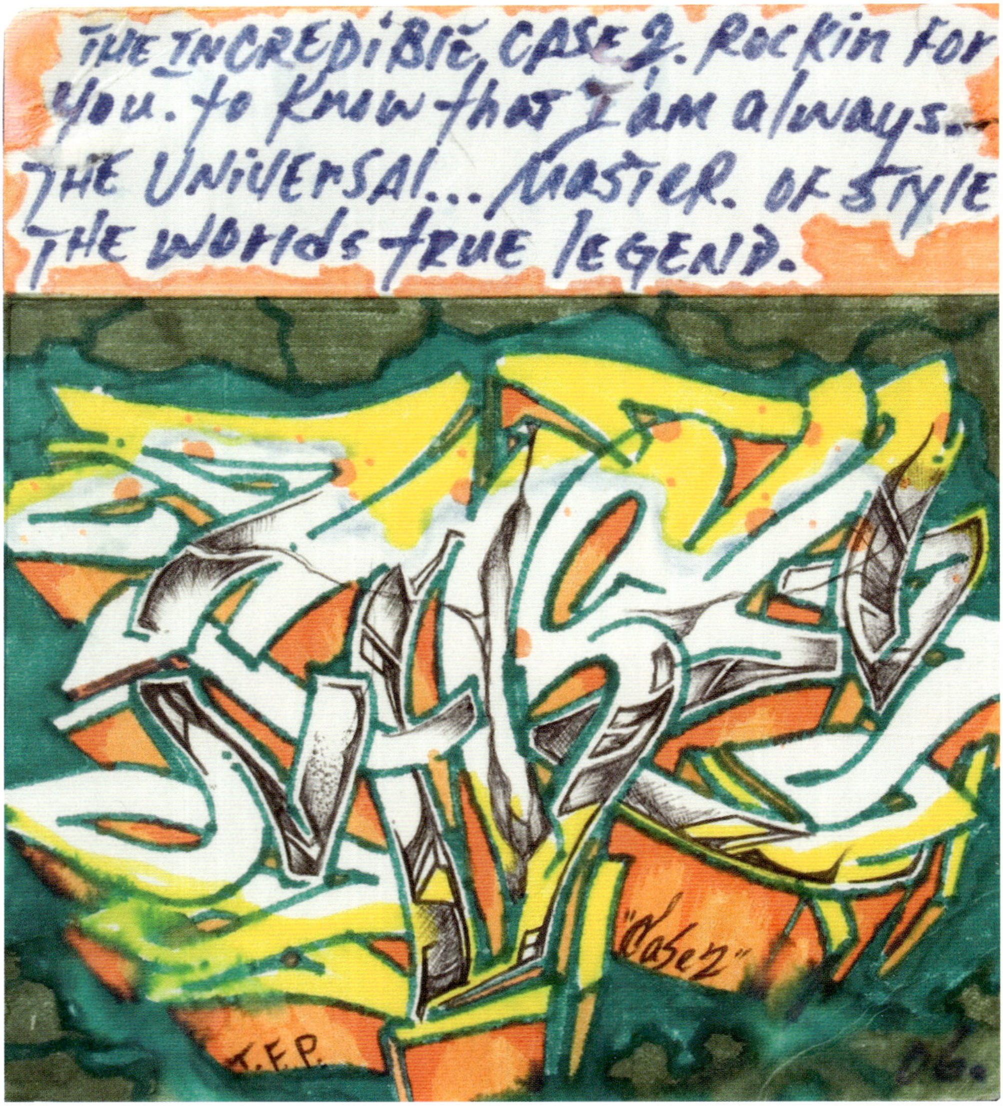
THE INCREDIBLE, CASE 2. ROCKIN FOR
YOU. TO KNOW THAT I AM ALWAYS..
THE UNIVERSAL... MASTER. OF STYLE
THE WORLDS TRUE LEGEND.
"Case 2"
T.F.P.
06.

KASE2

Kase2 (also known as Case2) was a graffiti style master and pioneer from the Bronx. Born Jeff Brown in 1958, Kase2 died in 2011 after a prodigious career that he kept exclusively to the streets. He painted his first wall in 1973 and by 1976 he was creating masterpieces on Bronx subway trains alongside the TFP crew. He later joined the TDS crew, who at the time were creating the most impressive art on trains, and with his partner Butch2 continued to develop his own original style.

Known for his street style and swagger, Kase2 became a significant force in the subway movement, collaborating with the best artists of the early 1980s. During this time he created a style of lettering that he dubbed 'computer rock', with letters separated into pieces and layering over each other in a complex shape.

Kase2 had a natural flair and talent for mentorship and over his lifetime he mentored many artists, including Phade, Nome, Moet, Bem, Sento and Ease. It was this unselfish and generous nature that furthered his popularity among his peers. However, he was also regarded as a tough figure, troubled by a precarious existence that had him in and out of prison for the majority of his life. During those many years in prison he continued to draw and share his lettering style with his protégés, ensuring that his own style lived on.

***Left*:** Kase2, untitled prison drawing, ink on cigarette carton, 2009. Collection of KET.

***Below*:** Real (Kase2) and Butch2, whole car, Bronx, New York, USA, 1980. Photographer unknown.

Above: Much (Kase2), New Design High School, New York, USA, 2009. Photography by KET.
Below: Kase2 in action, Bronx, New York, USA, 2007. Photography by KET.
Right: Much (Kase2), black book drawing, ink on paper, 23 x 30 c.m., 1983. Museum of the City of New York / Martin Wong Collection.
Right below: Butch2 and Kase2, whole car subway train, New York, USA, *c*. late 1970s. Photographer unknown.

LEGENDARY STATUS

As a boy, Kase2 lost both an arm and a leg, but regardless of his handicap he was considered one of the best and fiercest writers to come from the Bronx.

LADY PINK

Lady Pink (Sandra Fabara) was born in 1964 in Ecuador and raised in New York City. In 1979, while at the city's High School of Art and Design, she started writing graffiti and painting subways, and was one of the few women in the heavily male-dominated subculture. During her high-school years she was already exhibiting paintings in galleries, and at the age of twenty-one had her first solo show at the Moore College of Art and Design in Philadelphia. As one of the acknowledged leaders in the rise of graffiti-based art, Lady Pink's works have been embraced by important art collections, such as those of the Brooklyn Museum, the Whitney Museum, the Metropolitan Museum of Art in New York City, and the Groninger Museum in the Netherlands. Now firmly established in the fine arts world, her paintings are highly prized by collectors.

Today she runs a mural company with her husband, the artist Smith, creating large works around New York City. Together, they constitute one of the few professional teams to originate from the graffiti subculture. She shares her twenty years of experience by holding mural workshops with teens and lecturing at colleges throughout the United States.

LEGENDARY STATUS

Lady Pink played a starring role in the motion picture *Wild Style* in 1983, and became a global cult figure in the hip-hop world.

***Previous pages*:** Lady Pink, untitled mural with Smith, Muse and Cycle, Brooklyn, New York, USA, 1995. Photography by KET.

***Far left*:** Lady Pink, whole car on the CC train, Brooklyn, New York, USA, 1983. Photography by artist.

***Left*:** Lady Pink, *5Pointz Fairy*, Queens, New York, USA, 2008. Photography by artist.

***Below*:** Lady Pink, mural, Queens, New York, USA, 1996. Photography by KET.

LEE

Born in Ponce, Puerto Rico, in 1960, Lee Quiñones was raised in New York City's Lower East Side in a family that kept close ties to their cultural heritage, surrounded by a predominantly Nuyorican (New York Puerto Rican) community.

He gravitated towards the urban underground during the explosive 1970s and in late 1975 Lee began creating whole 12-metre (40-foot) subway car murals and was asked to join the Fabulous Five, an elite quintet of almost mythic graffiti writers. Over the next decade he would paint an estimated 115 whole subway cars throughout the transit system.

Among his many accomplishments, Lee was instrumental in moving elaborate graffiti art above ground when he stealthily painted *Howard the Duck*, the first entire 7.5 x 9 metre (25 x 30 foot) handball court mural, in the spring of 1978 outside his high school, which set the blueprint for handball court murals in New York City.

Lee is considered by many to be the single most influential artist to emerge from the New York City subway art movement. Celebrated in both the contemporary art world and in popular culture circles, he is dedicated to producing work that provokes reactions and challenges the status quo.

***Far left*:** Lee, *Benchmark: A Great Rush Hour in the Bronx*, oil paint, charcoal pencil and spray paint on linen, 274 x 426 c.m., 2011. Image courtesy of KET.

***Top*:** Lee, whole car, New York, USA, 1979. Image courtesy of KET.

***Above*:** Lee, *Hagar the Horrible* whole car, New York, USA, *c*. 1978. Image courtesy of KET.

***Left*:** Lee, untitled, acrylic and spray paint on canvas, 120 x 130 c.m., 1982. Speerstra Collection.

LOOMIT

Loomit (Mathias Köhler, born in 1968 in Celle, Germany) began his graffiti career in 1983; he was introduced to hip-hop and graffiti through a schoolmate's older sister after she returned from a trip to New York City. From that time on his life was filled with 'style'. It took him just one summer to bomb all available walls in his small town. Fortunately, the decision by his mother to move to Munich opened up a much wider playground.

In 1986 Loomit narrowly avoided prison time after he was prosecuted for vandalism. However, his ambition would not be so easily discouraged, and in the following years he created hundreds of murals, setting a new standard for graffiti mural productions wordwide, and establishing the largest legal outdoor space for artists to paint in Europe – it became known as a Hall of Fame (locations maintained by the graffiti community where the best artists can paint without fear of prosecution).

Loomit is known for the immense scale of his work; his three-dimensional lettering style, which unlike most traditional graffiti lettering changes proportion and size drastically within the piece; and his fish-eye perspective murals. He is part of the first wave of globetrotting graffiti artists (along with ATOME, Drax, Milk, Kasino, Egs, Delta, Zebster and others) to explore and paint in cities not previously known to have had graffiti, and thus break new ground and influence new artists.

LEGENDARY STATUS

In 1996, collaborating with Daim, Darco, Hesh, Ohne and Vaine, Loomit created the tallest graffiti mural in the world in Bergedorf.

Above: HEX and Loomit, *LA to Germany*, Los Angeles, California, USA, 1991. Photography by Charlie DTK.

Left: Loomit, Naestved, Denmark, 2014. Image courtesy of artist.

MODE 2

Mode 2 was born on the small island of Mauritius in 1967, moved to London in 1976, and fell into hip-hop in the summer of 1984. He got hooked by watching the opening scene of the US high-school series *Welcome Back, Kotter*, and after seeing the graffiti artist Dondi painting in the 'Buffalo Gals' music video. As a result, he picked up the marker pen and can of paint not so much for the illegality, but more so because he was fascinated by what these new tools could do.

After trying to write and create characters like those he had seen in New York City, he decided that he should make his own style, by using his own cultural reference points. He thus set about carving out his own individual niche in the spray-painting culture, focusing on his own characters in combination with the New York City tradition of letter dynamics that he had fallen in love with.

Mode 2 is not only motivated by writing, but by hip-hop in general, and he supports various dance events, including Battle of the Year, which is the world's largest b-boy competition and has been held annually in Germany since 1990.

Below: Mode 2, *Amigos*, Valencia, Spain, 2013. Photography by artist.
Top right: Mode 2, *Loud 'N' Proud*, Athens, Greece, 2009. Photography by artist.
Right: Mode 2, Strasbourg, France, 2010. Image courtesy of artist.

LOUD 'N' PROUD
FAMILY FIRST...

PISTE DE
LA METZGERAU
Neudorf
ONE LINERS
WRITERS

***Far left*:** Nick Walker, *Liberty*, Paris, France, 2014. Photography by artist.
***Left*:** Nick Walker, *Moona Lisa*, spray paint on canvas, 75 x 56 c.m., 2006. Private collection.
***Following pages left top*:** Nick Walker, *Vandal*, Bristol, UK, 2011. Photography by artist.
***Following pages left bottom*:** Nick Walker, *I Love NY*, New York, USA, 2012. Photography by KET.
***Following pages right*:** Nick Walker, *Vandal Girl*, New York, USA, 2012. Photography by KET.

NICK WALKER

Nick Walker (born in 1969) is one of the most famous street artists. Emerging from the groundbreaking Bristol graffiti scene of the early 1980s, Nick would go on to become a forerunner of the British graffiti phenomenon. His work is constantly evolving, with new methods and new messages, and has become a blueprint for success for hundreds of aspiring artists, including – perhaps most famously – Banksy.

With expert precision, Nick combines the freedom of the spray can with very controlled and intricate stencilling, drawing on the raw energy and imagery of graffiti but always creating something innovative and unique. The methods he uses also retain their gravity and integrity when transferred to the traditional medium of canvas.

Over the course of his long career, Nick's work has been praised by the media and has attracted headlines worldwide. In 2008 he had sell-out shows in Los Angeles and London, where collectors queued for over twenty-four hours to be among the first to get their hands on his latest works. In the same year, his iconic painting *Moona Lisa* sold for £54,000, over ten times its estimated value, at auction at Bonhams in London.

LEGENDARY STATUS

Nick was commissioned by Stanley Kubrick to recreate the graffiti-laden streets of New York City for the set of *Eyes Wide Shut*.

24 HOUR ELECTRONIC PROTECTION
SECURETECH
SECURITY SYSTEMS INC.
718-726-7811

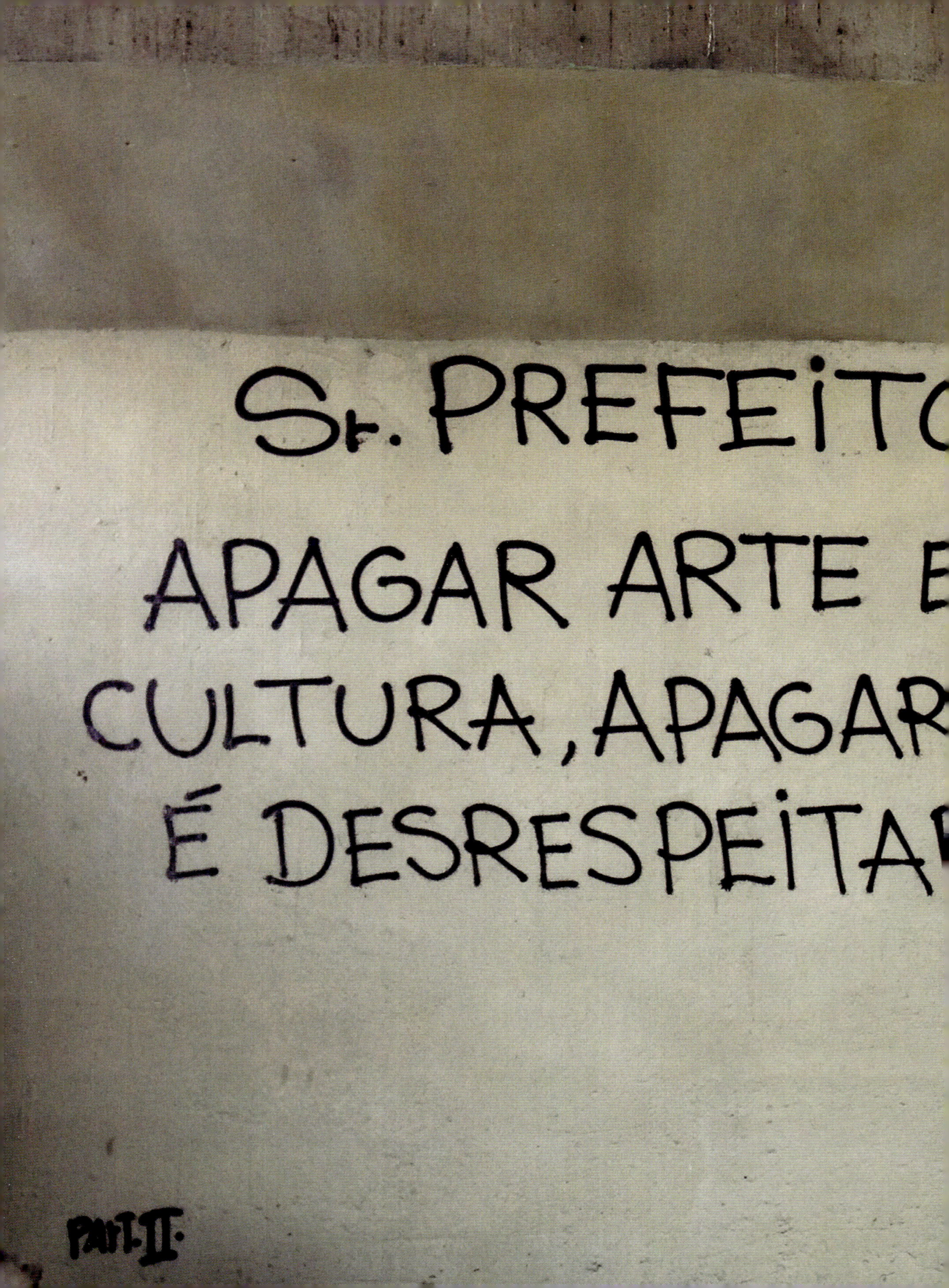
Sr. PREFEIT
APAGAR ARTE
CULTURA, APAGAR
É DESRESPEITA
PART.II.

OSGEMEOS

Born in São Paulo, Brazil, in 1974, OSGEMEOS are the twin brothers Gustavo and Otavio Pandolfo (OSGEMEOS translates as THETWINS). As children, they developed a different way to play and communicate through art, and with the arrival of hip-hop culture in Brazil in the 1980s, the transition into graffiti came very naturally, as they explored various techniques of painting, drawing and sculpture, and used the streets as their canvas.

In Brazil they became known as much for their murals as for their duotone throw-ups (in bold yellow with red outlines), which still to this day spread across São Paulo. Their characters – yellow skinned and

***Previous pages*:** OSGEMEOS, street painting, São Paulo, Brazil, 2015. Image courtesy of artist.
***Above*:** OSGEMEOS, luggage store gallery mural, San Francisco, USA, 2013.
Image courtesy of artist.
***Right*:** OSGEMEOS and Futura, Chelsea, New York, USA, 2010. Photography by 12ozProphet.

adorned with clothes inspired by Brazilian folklore, or sometimes nude with only shirts doubling as ski masks – are staples in the streets of their home town and spring up in the cities they touch down in. Over the years these figures have grown in size and have been used in some of OSGEMEOS' most iconic and fantastic murals. Towering over several districts (in Boston, New York City, San Francisco, Berlin and Lisbon, among others), they have at times caused upset with their sheer visual impact.

In 2005 OSGEMEOS were invited to paint the first authorized whole train in Brazil. The project had them painting entire train cars with fellow VLOK crew members and special guests such as Doze Green and Reas. Whole trains, done legally or illegally, are every graffiti writer's dream, and this particular project raised the twins to an even greater level of recognition.

Over the years, the artistic world created by the duo has surpassed their work in the streets and has become a language in itself, constantly absorbing new cultures and new adventures. They are admired internationally for using their combined visual language and improvisation, and for developing and sharing their playful world in various projects around the globe.

RETNA

Retna (Marquis Lewis, born in 1979) initially turned to graffiti writing as an alternative to the gang culture that was present in his community. He soon became a dedicated writer, whose name was visible on freeways and walls across Los Angeles. He also developed an original method for creating wildstyle pieces that ensured his gigantic murals and other works would stand out from the competition.

In the mid 2000s, Retna joined many of his crew mates in making the transition to fine art and murals. His murals with El Mac, which appeared throughout Los Angeles and the Americas, firmly established him as a world-class muralist and transported him to a new level of popularity. Many of his pieces synthesize fine art and graffiti, and use his ornate painting technique that mixes paintbrushes with the traditional spray can. His art is filled with stories and includes his own self-created alphabet, which is a hybrid of global fonts: Cholo graffiti, Egyptian, Asian, Hebrew, Arabic, hieroglyphic and ink calligraphy.

Today, Retna travels between the galleries and streets with ease as a member of the internationally exclusive art collective the Seventh Letter, a group that has influenced contemporary art on a global scale.

Below: Retna, *Sacred Dance of Memories (Salva los Espiritus Santos)*, Wynwood Walls, Miami, Florida, USA, 2012. Photography by KET.

Right bottom: Retna, *Brimstone*, Miami, Florida, USA, 2012. Photography by KET.

Above: Retna, *Retna*, acrylic on canvas, 1.52 x 50.8 m., Silver Lining exhibit, Primary Flight gallery, Miami, Florida, USA, 2010. Photography by KET.

LEGENDARY STATUS

In 1989 Risk travelled to New York City to paint subway trains with JA, Ghost, Ven, Reas and KET, becoming the first Los Angeles writer ever to paint subway trains.

RISK

Risk (Kelly Graval) is a graffiti and fine artist whose art has been synonymous with Los Angeles for decades. He has come a long way since he pioneered the painting of freeway overpasses, signs and billboards, dubbed 'heavens', practising a uniquely clean and legible style. Together with his painting partner SLICK, Risk has painted some of Los Angeles' most elaborate and stylized murals, as part of the aptly named crew Aerosolics. Fame in the graffiti world came when he and SLICK travelled to England in 1989 to compete in the Bridlington International Street Art Competition and won first place.

Risk is also co-founder of the West Coast Artists crew, and has made an indelible impression on the Los Angeles landscape with art that moves from highways to freight trains to canvases, and massive street murals that bring new life into their communities.

As his fame grew around the Los Angeles art community, it didn't take long for Risk to become a hot commodity in the music scene. His art appears in an impressive array of bands' music videos, from the Red Hot Chili Peppers and Ice Cube to Bad

Above: Risk, Cloverfield mural, Santa Monica, California, USA, 2015. Photography by Bird Man.
Right: Risk, Los Angeles, California, USA, 1991. Photography by artist.

Religion and Michael Jackson. Risk has also worked for some of the most notable music festivals, musicians and events around the globe, including Coachella, the MTV Music Awards, the Doors and Aerosmith.

Risk's entrepreneurial spirit and desire to push creative concepts ultimately spawned the first authentic line of graffiti-inspired clothing, Third Rail, one of the hottest clothing brands to emerge from Southern California.

Although Risk loves aerosol art, he sees it as merely one genre in his life's work. From his days as a student at the USC Roski School of Fine Arts in Los Angeles to gallery and museum showings around the world, Risk has transformed from a graffiti artist to a rising star in the contemporary art world, showcasing his art across the globe, and generating media attention along the way. To this day, he continues to break down barriers in both art and commerce, while remaining grounded and respectful of the culture he contributes to. At present, Risk stays connected to his roots by supporting artists and giving back to the community through numerous charitable endeavours.

***Above*:** Risk and SMASH 137, Miami, Florida, USA, 2010. Photography by artist.

***Below*:** Risk, bus piece, Los Angeles, California, USA, 2011. Image courtesy of artist.

***Right*:** Risk, Riskrock WC, Santa Monica, California, USA, 2015. Photography by Bird Man.

RISKROCK

***Above*:** ROA, squirrels, Brooklyn, New York, USA, 2012. Photography by KET.

***Right*:** ROA, rabbit, Cordy House, Shoreditch, London, UK, 2010. Photography by Yves Cosentino.

ROA

ROA is a prolific Belgian street artist known for his gigantic murals of animals and birds. His depictions of the animals include versions where they are partly dissected, their internal organs exposed or their skeletal system entirely visible. The impact on passers-by has generated a great deal of attention for ROA and he has been able to spread his work far and wide, from his home town of Ghent to Newcastle in the UK, Berlin, Vietnam, Mexico City, Cambodia and Poland. Each work is tailored to its location and takes into account the surrounding environment and local species.

ROA has participated in many mural festivals, such as the Cologne CityLeaks Festival in Germany, the Bristol See No Evil street art festival in the UK, Komafest in Norway, Los Muros Hablan in Puerto Rico and the Wall Therapy festival in Rochester, New York.

His studio paintings are generally painted on found objects and, like his murals, depict animal subjects.

CIAL
PATRIOT
EMISSION ACCOMPLISH
CIAL
INACTION
PACE
CLIMAT

LEGENDARY STATUS

Robbie is considered one of the US's leading satirical street poster artists, and in 1989 received a National Endowment for the Arts Individual Artist grant in order to pursue his work further.

***Far left*:** Robbie Conal, *Patriot Inaction* and other posters, Los Angeles, California, USA, 2011. Photography by KET.
***Left*:** Robbie Conal, *Contra Cocaine* poster, 74 x 58 c.m., 2011. Robbie Conal collection.

ROBBIE CONAL

Robbie Conal (born in 1944) was brought up on the Upper West Side of Manhattan. His parents were union organizers who believed that a young mind was better developed outside the day care centre and instead immersed him in the great art institutions of New York City. Conal attended the city's High School of Music and Art, and later received his Bachelor of Fine Arts from San Francisco State University in 1969, and his Masters of Fine Arts from Stanford University in 1978.

In 1986, angered by what he saw as the Reagan administration's radical abuse of power, he began designing satirical oil portraits of politicians and bureaucrats, which he would then turn into street posters. Conal gradually attracted an army of volunteers, who helped him poster the streets of major cities around the country, and his work has escalated from there. Over the past twenty-four years, he has made more than eighty different street posters satirizing politicians, both Republicans and Democrats, televangelists and global capitalists. His work has also tackled subjects like censorship, war, social injustice and environmental issues.

Conal's work has been featured by most major US media outlets, and the *Washington Post* has dubbed him 'America's foremost street artist'.

ROBBO

Prior to the New York City-inspired graffiti explosion in the mid 1980s, John Robertson (1969–2014), aka ROBBO, was already writing an abbreviated version of his surname on the streets of London. ROBBO was a skinhead and a football fan who wrote his nickname and that of his team, Arsenal, all over his school, the housing estate where he lived, and in and around the football stadiums where Arsenal played their matches. He wrote for fun and knew nothing of the wider graffiti subculture. Then, around 1984, he saw the documentary *Style Wars* (1983) and everything changed. Without hesitation he embraced this new 'stylized' version of what he was already doing and became a 'graffiti writer'.

As the 1990s dawned, ROBBO started to travel and paint around Europe. Then in 1992 he painted on the New York City subway. Having fulfilled this lifelong dream, he returned to London and put his art on the back burner in order to raise a family.

Throughout this period ROBBO's oldest piece (*Robbo Incorporated*, painted in 1985) had remained partially unscathed on a wall in Camden, gaining cult status in the London graffiti world as no other piece of graffiti from the mid 1980s had managed to survive. Controversy hit when the street artist Banksy chose to incorporate this painting into a new piece of work. It wasn't clear whether Banksy deliberately targeted ROBBO, but as soon as ROBBO heard the news, the old 'King of London' was back with a vengeance. An art war raged across the graffiti world, as graffiti writers rallied to ROBBO's side. They attacked the works of Banksy who was seen as a usurper of a scene that they had created, and the slogan 'TEAM ROBBO' was pasted on streets the world over.

***Top*:** Banksy's appropriation of ROBBO's work, *Robbo incorporated*, Camden, London, UK, 2009. Image courtesy of Zak Hussein/PA Wire/Press Association Images.

***Above*:** ROBBO's retaliation, Camden, London, UK, 2010. Photography by Teamrobbo.org.

***Left*:** ROBBO, *Robster*, Amsterdam, Holland, 1992. Photography by Drax.

SABER

Among the thousands of people who make up the graffiti and street art community around the world, there are few names that carry the same weight as that of Saber. Born in the Los Angeles suburb of Glendale in 1976, Saber was raised by creative parents and he discovered his passion for art at an early age. At thirteen, his cousins took him to see the spray paint-covered Belmont Tunnel. From that moment on, graffiti became his whole life. After honing his skills he joined the infamous MSK crew, and was later inducted into the legendary piecing crew AWR.

Saber was already a fixture on the Los Angeles graffiti scene by 1997, when he completed the largest graffiti piece ever created. Located on the sloping cement bank of the Los Angeles River, it was nearly the size of a professional football field, and took 125 gallons of paint and 35 nights to complete. In a famous photograph – taken by his father just after it was finished – Saber stands on the piece and appears as a tiny speck amid

a giant blaze of colour. It catapulted him to legend status in the graffiti world.

In 2010 Saber released a video in which the year's heated healthcare debate in the US was spray painted over the American flag. While some saw it as desecration, others appreciated his call for healthcare reform and his honesty in revealing that he had epilepsy and was therefore uninsurable. This work led him to create a large group of American flag paintings called the 'Tarnished' series. Also in 2010, Saber took to the skies of Los Angeles to make a visual protest against the city's policies on banning legal murals. This massive spectacle, in which Saber used skywriting to make statements that could be seen across the city, was an extraordinary success and forced Los Angeles' policies to be reviewed. This campaign was one of the first of its kind to integrate social media directly from the skies. Ever since, Saber has been extremely active via Twitter, raising awareness about the causes he is passionate about.

Previous pages left: Saber, detail of wall painted with OSGEMEOS, Retna, Revok, Norm, and Rime, Hollywood, Los Angeles, California, USA, 2011. Photography by Saber.
Previous pages right: Saber, *Lo'se*, mixed mediums on canvas, 122 x 104 c.m., 2010. Image courtesy of artist.

***Above*:** Saber, LA River mural, 125 gallons of roller paint illegally painted, 17 x 76 m., Los Angeles, California, USA, 1997. Image courtesy of artist.

***Below*:** Saber, *Green Monster*, Los Angeles, California, USA, 2010. Image courtesy of artist.

LEGENDARY STATUS

Sane Smith became notorious for painting on the top level of New York City's Brooklyn Bridge, after which they were sued by the City for $3 million, the biggest lawsuit to date against graffiti writers. The work was visible for miles.

Top: Sane Smith, Broom Hilda wall, New York, USA, 1990. Image courtesy of artist.
Middle: Sane Smith, Smith Sane wall, New York, USA, 1986. Image courtesy of artist.
Bottom: Sane Smith, Brooklyn Bridge pieces, New York, USA, 1988. Image courtesy of artist.
Right: Sane Smith, JFK Exp. RIP, train panel, New York, USA, 1989. Image courtesy of artist.

SANE SMITH

The name of Sane Smith has appeared on the streets of New York City for over thirty years. Originally Sane Smith were two brothers, Roger Smith ('Smith') and the late David Smith ('Sane'), who were raised in the Washington Heights district of Manhattan, where New York City tagging was born.

During the heyday of train painting in the 1980s, the brothers were responsible for introducing the use of house paint to cover trains, as an alternative to spray paint that was in common use at the time. This innovation was widely adopted by artists in the 1990s and is a favourite even to this day.

In 1990, after David tragically drowned in Flushing Bay in New York City, Roger continued to paint – using the name that he had shared with his brother – with as much vigour and determination as ever. At a time when many writers concentrated on painting walls, Roger Smith took to doing it all: he was an early figure in freight train painting before it was adopted nationwide, a proponent of style writing through his association with the TDS crew, and a contributor to many mural productions with his own crew and his wife, the artist Lady Pink.

Now in his forties, Roger Smith remains a writer's writer who stays out of the limelight, and who paints for his own enjoyment.

SHEPARD FAIREY

Shepard Fairey (born in 1970) is the artist behind OBEY GIANT, a graphics style and collection that has changed the way people see art and the urban landscape. The story begins in 1989 at the Rhode Island School of Design in Providence, where Fairey received his Bachelor of Fine Arts in Illustration and created the 'Andre the Giant has a Posse' sticker. Having gained recognition from posting the stickers around his local area, his project was such a success that it ultimately transformed into the OBEY GIANT art campaign. Although the campaign is rooted in the DIY counterculture of punk rock and skateboarding, it has also taken cues from popular culture, commercial marketing and political messaging. Fairey steeps his ideology and iconography in the self-empowerment of those who refuse to be manipulated by the machine of

Please no graffiti up here.
Thank you, Paul Richard

LEGENDARY STATUS

In 2008, Fairey's 'Hope' portrait was lauded as the single key image of Barack Obama's presidential campaign. It can now be found in the Smithsonian's National Portrait Gallery.

Previous pages left: Shepard Fairey, *Lotus Woman* mural, Dumbo, Brooklyn, New York, USA, 2013. Photography by Noel Y. C.
Previous pages right: Shepard Fairey, Brooklyn, New York, USA, 2010. Photography by KET.
Above: Shepard Fairey, *Andre the Giant* poster, Miami, Florida, USA, 2010. Photography by KET.

Right: Shepard Fairey, *Peace Tree* mural, the Line Hotel, Los Angeles, California, USA, 2014. Photography by Phil Liff-Grieff.

manufactured consent. With biting sarcasm that is verging on reverse psychology, he goads viewers, using the imperative 'obey', to take heed of the propagandists who are out to bend the world to their agendas.

In addition to his guerrilla street art presence, Fairey has executed more than forty-three large-scale painted public murals around the world. His works are in the permanent collections of the Museum of Modern Art in New York City, the Victoria and Albert Museum in London, the Smithsonian's National Portrait Gallery in Washington, DC, the Institute of Contemporary Art in Boston, the San Francisco Museum of Modern Art and many others.

PEACE

SHOE

Niels Shoe Meulman (born in 1967) is an internationally known artist, raised in Amsterdam, where he is still based. He began tagging as 'Shoe' when he was just twelve, and became a graffiti legend by the time he was eighteen. In the 1980s he met influential New York City artists Dondi, Rammellzee and Keith Haring, and was invited to join the CIA crew, an honour bestowed on a rare few by style master Dondi. He went on to form his own international crew, the Crime Time Kings, with graffiti artists Bando from Paris and Mode 2 from London. Together they helped graffiti develop its own distinctive style in Europe and influenced thousands of artists across the world.

In the 1990s Shoe expanded his skills by apprenticing under the Dutch graphic artist Anthon Beeke. In the following years, he ran his own design company, Caulfield & Tensing, and was partner in advertising agency Unruly, which he later turned into a brand for silk scarves and a gallery showcasing new artists.

Shoe has continued to explore the art of graffiti writing, and in 2007 he came up with the idea of 'Calligraffiti', an art form that fuses calligraphy and graffiti. Since then, his calligraphic paintings (signed NSM) have been shown in many international exhibitions and are part of several museum collections.

Left: Niels Shoe Meulman, featuring cassowary bird, Mays Lane, Sydney, Australia, 2012. Photography by Adele Renault.

Above: Niels Shoe Meulman, *Welcome to Amsterdam* mural at Club Trouw, Amsterdam, Holland, 2012. Photography by Bas Uterwijk.

Below: Niels Shoe Meulman in action, Helsinki, Finland, 2014. Image courtesy of the artist.

Left: Slick, Dissizit! LA Hands logo, 2015. Image courtesy of artist.
Above: Slick, Belmont Yard, Los Angeles, California, USA, 1994. Photography by Charlie DTK.
Following pages left: Slick, Dissizit!, Los Angeles, California, USA, 2007. Image courtesy of artist.
Following pages top right: Slick, detail from the Slick and Hex battle, Los Angeles, California, USA, 1990. Photography by Charlie DTK.
Following pages, bottom: Slick and Dream SMD, detail from site-specific installation at MOCA, Los Angeles, California, USA, 2012. Photography by KET.

SLICK

Slick (born in 1967) began his rise to the top in the mid 1980s when he started painting on the streets of his hometown of Honolulu, Hawaii. Later, he moved to Pasadena, California, where he studied at the Art Center College of Design during the day while painting LA's walls by night.

The televised 'Slick vs. Hex' graffiti battle was a pivotal moment in Slick's career; he went from underground hell raiser to garnering worldwide acclaim. This international attention opened many doors for Slick, and his work found its way to music videos, feature films, album covers and even established gallery exhibits. It was also during this time that he realized the potential of reaching a much larger audience by putting his art on T-shirts. Since his first designs in the late 1980s, Slick has designed graphics for the likes of Stussy, X-Large, Adidas and Obey – and the

LEGENDARY STATUS

Slick created the album artwork for the classic Pharcyde hip-hop album *Bizarre Ride II the Pharcyde*.

list goes on. His graphic design aesthetic has influenced an entire generation of artists and designers; he even pioneered a movement called 'street wear' long before the phrase came into popular use.

Slick's main focus nowadays is his clothing brand, Dissizit! Over the past twelve years, Dissizit! has established itself as a brand not to be taken lightly, with a take-no-prisoners attitude to its assault on pop culture. The brand's distinctive 'LA Hands' logo has become a de facto symbol for Los Angeles pride.

Whether it's painting a mural, designing a sports shoe, formulating a paint scheme for a car, art directing graffiti for a video game, creating a collection for Dissizit!, or signing his name for a fan, Slick treats each and every single thing he touches as a work of art that's worthy of his name.

SLICK

#33
ONCE UPON
A DRIVE-BY
BELMONT
TUNNEL

Above: Stephen Powers, *Stay Up*, Johannesburg, South Africa, 2012. Photography by Martha Cooper.
Right: Stephen Powers, *Euphoria Bridge*, Brooklyn, New York, USA, 2012. Photography by KET.

STEPHEN POWERS

Stephen Powers (aka ESPO), a former graffiti artist turned muralist, sign painter and fine artist, is a Philadelphia native who has put his mark on many houses and buildings around the world. In 1999 Powers stopped writing graffiti and tending bar to dedicate himself to the life of a full-time artist. The commitment paid off and his work has been shown at contemporary art festivals around the world, such as the Venice and Liverpool Biennials, as well as in multiple shows at the Deitch Projects gallery in New York City. In 2007 Powers was awarded a Fulbright scholarship to paint in the streets of Dublin and Belfast. His work in Belfast's Lower Shankill area was inspired by the area's political murals, and Powers told *The New York Times* that he was 'taking the form of the murals, which are powerful for all the wrong reasons, and trying to retain some of the power and use it in a really good way'.

In Philadelphia, in 2010, building on what he had started in Ireland, Powers began working on an ongoing mural project about the complexities and rewards of relationships, titled *A Love Letter for You*. These days Powers continues to bring great murals and signs to communities around the world, and operates his own art/sign shop in Brooklyn, New York City.

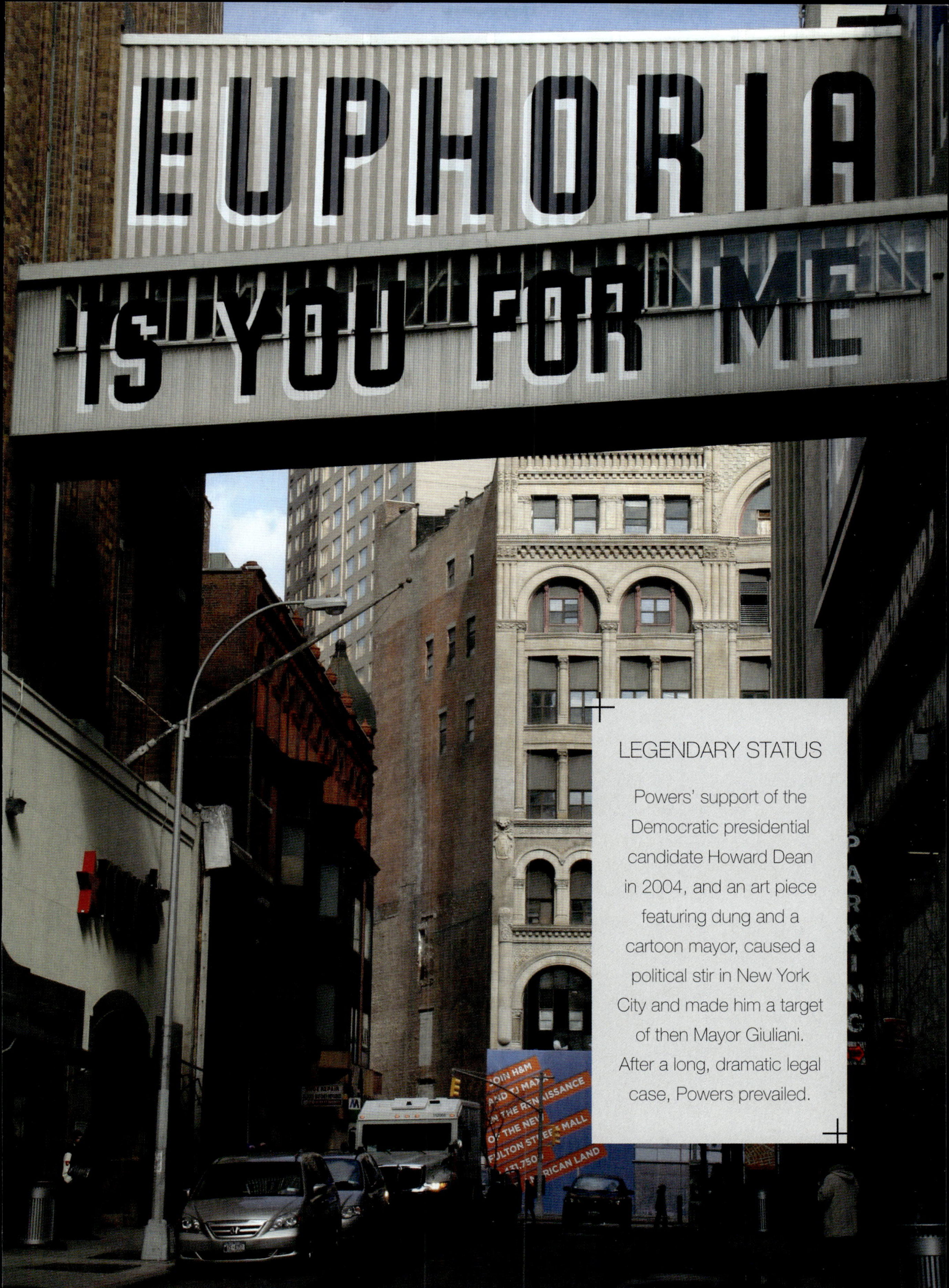

LEGENDARY STATUS

Powers' support of the Democratic presidential candidate Howard Dean in 2004, and an art piece featuring dung and a cartoon mayor, caused a political stir in New York City and made him a target of then Mayor Giuliani. After a long, dramatic legal case, Powers prevailed.

T-KID 170

T-KID 170 (Julius Cavero, born in 1961) started his career in 1974 as a street tagger for his neighbourhood gang, the Bronx Enchanters, and later for the Renegades of Harlem. After getting shot in 1977, he transformed his life in order to get away from the dangers of gang life: he took on the name T-KID 170 and fully embraced his vocation as a graffiti artist painting subway trains. During the late 1970s and early 1980s, T-KID 170 helped create some of the most elaborate and complex train pieces of the time.

T-KID 170 eventually quit painting trains and started to exhibit his work in major gallery shows and collections, starting with the Sam Esses collection in 1979. From then on he painted with all the major players, including Cope2, Part One, Bio, Kongo and Ces, and was part of Fashion Moda's exhibition in 1980, where the Sidney Janis Gallery asked him to be part of their worldwide exhibition. In 1981 he was involved in the PS1 show, where photos of his art on trains were exhibited with such greats as the group SAMO (aka Jean-Michel Basquiat, Keith Haring and Lee Quiñones).

Left**:** SHOCK, T-KID 170, CEM, whole car, Bronx, New York, USA, *c*. 1981. Photography by Henry Chalfant.

Left below**:** T-KID 170, *MOTUG* wall, Brooklyn, New York, USA, 2010. Photography by KET.

Below**:** T-KID 170, Graffiti Hall of Fame, East Harlem, New York, USA, 2003. Photography by KET.

LEGENDARY STATUS

T-KID 170 featured as a character in Marc Ecko's video game 'Getting Up: Contents Under Pressure'.

TRACY 168

Tracy 168 (Michael Tracy, born in 1958) is a pioneering visual artist who began his urban-art journey in 1969 as a young boy writing his name in and around his native Manhattan. As his talents progressed, he discovered the power of painting the subway trains as a means of getting his name known in the graffiti art community. It changed his life and made him a major figure in the growing train-painting movement. During the early 1970s, Tracy 168 painted hundreds of pieces in many different styles, and in 1973 he introduced the notion of painting cartoons on trains. He was also the founder of the influential Wanted crew, and when the crew disbanded in 1975 he founded Wild Style, a crew of talented subway painters who embodied the true meaning of the term 'wild style' with their elaborate, intricate and visionary approach. Tracy 168's accomplishments are many and include selling custom works painted onto the side of trains to New Yorkers, introducing large-scale street memorial murals to honour the deceased, and becoming the first commercial graffiti artist commissioned to paint murals for businesses around New York City.

Above: Tracy 168, untitled, spray paint on canvas, 91 x 152 c.m., 2012. Collection of KET.
Below: BILLY 167 and Tracy 168, end-to-end on New York City subway car, Bronx, New York, USA, 1980. Photography by SACH.

LEGENDARY STATUS

In the 1970s Tracy 168 painted the colours (jackets) for many well-known New York gangs, such as the Reapers, Bachelors, Tomahawks, Savage Skulls and the Ministers.

Above: OSGEMEOS, Vancouver Biennale mural, Vancouver, Canada, 2014. Image courtesy of artist.

THANK YOU

Special thanks to my wife, Andrea, for being patient and handling the baby duties while I worked long nights (love you Aya and Jasmine). And to my two oldest children, Talia and Xolo, for also being supportive of me and my work.

Many thanks to Freedom, DOC TC5, Fuzz One, Mode 2, Wane One, Cost, Ezo, Part One and Tracy 168 who listened to me and gave me valuable input.

Thanks to Luna Park and Ray Mock for the image support.

And thanks to Revs for putting in so much work in New York City, your contribution to the book is missed.

This book is dedicated to the memory of the legends: Iz the Wiz, Kase2, DG, Sane, Pnut 2, Dondi and Stayhigh 149.

2008
THE DEATH SQUAD